YOLITA

The Lectures of Thumbert Thumbert

By John B. Nearly

With an Introduction by
Scott W. Webb

Dedicated to the memory of John F. Kennedy,
who didn't see it coming.

And the eyes of them both were opened,
and they knew that they were naked.
Genesis 3:7

Table of Contents

Introduction to John Nearly's *Yolita*

The Lectures of Thumbert Thumbert

By Scott W. Webb

Part One

The two men in this photo are actors James Mason (right) and Jerry Stovin (adjusting Mason's tie); Mason played the lead protagonist in the film, *Lolita* (1962), as Dr. Humbert Humbert. Jerry Stovin played John Farlow, husband to Jean, and father to Mona, Lolita's best friend.

This photo was helpful for me to appreciate the relationship between Humbert and John Farlow, which in truth, was a friendship far more complex, once I discovered in 2020 that these "fictional characters" were based upon actual, real people.

The next question might be: "Had the novelist and author of *Lolita*, Vladimir Nabokov, somehow previously *met* these two characters portrayed in his novel during his own life?"

No, he did not. Then how did Nabokov pattern his fiction to mirror the lives of real people he had never met? The answer is quite obvious, once we connect a few dots, which this book will explain in full detail. Like what had motivated Nabokov to write a novel about the mind of *a pedophile* which released in 1955? During the morally conservative Eisenhower period?

The missing link regarding Lolita's backstory is that Nabokov had *behind-the-scenes* backers. We could say that he was brought in as a ghost-writer, but more on that later.

Note the DISTANCE between Nabokov and the protagonist in *Lolita*. If Humbert's character was based upon a real person, could Nabokov have ADAPTED an actual, obscured memoir written by an author who was no longer living? And, not that it would matter, because *Lolita* as a work of fiction, stands entirely on its own.

It took me a while to piece "certain things" together, having stumbled onto the 1962 memoir, John Nearly's *Yolita*, which he self-published in 1963, just months prior to the assassination of President John F. Kennedy. *Yolita*, in context, provides a rare snapshot of American culture before everything changed November 22, 1963, interesting in its own right.

One other backdrop to note in this introduction, is the Cold War, which began almost immediately following WWII. Nabokov published *Lolita* in 1955, with Stanley Kubrick's adaptation to film releasing in 1962, at the HEIGHT of the Cold War period between the U.S. against China and the USSR.

Note the active involvement that U.S. Intelligence Services played to launch a *cultural war* between the West and the Soviet Union across this same period (1952-1962). Ask yourself, how such an inappropriate book as *Lolita* could be released at this time. And *why* was it published against all the odds?

What I mean to say, is that none of *Lolita's* publication makes any sense, unless we read John Nearly's account. If you are familiar with the film, you might assume that the fictional character of John Farlow in *Lolita* is insignificant; unless his secrets from 1962 were brought to light.

Obviously, I have had *nothing* to do with any of it, outside of a series of accidents which connected John Nearly to me, which I will explain as best I can. I myself am not a professional writer, nor was Mr. Nearly, so please bear with me and with him.

I do know: This incongruity of "pedophilia" presented to an unsuspecting public can't be solved from our current level of thinking. This is because we have been trained to look at the CONTENT within our minds as the primary formulation to our understanding; however, humanity has been misled. *Lolita* highlights how easily this can be done. And with the benefit of hindsight, we can better see how easily the public was likewise fooled regarding the now-obvious, deeper reality behind the Kennedy assassination in 1963.

Through the lectures of (the actual) French literature professor, Dr. Thumbert Thumbert, we can appreciate why he was censored, disgraced, in real life, and ultimately libeled. Like him, we will want to know how to break free from our captors, even more strange, because they have proven themselves to be more dishonorable than we are capable.

And certainly, we will learn that the Cold War was stripped of its veneer by Dr. Thumbert, who was purposefully silenced. And of course, we learn of his untimely death while still in prison, both in the Nabokov version and in the lost-version you now hold in your hands.

Part Two

I've noticed, and perhaps you have too, that things will happen in the world, which we miss.

And how would you know, that there is A GAP in the information which you have carefully compiled within your brain? For example, in the neighborhood where I was raised, there was a street named *Fairway* Lane, and to me, it was an ordinary residential street, so there was no *gap* in my mind that I knew of.

Years later, I learned that my neighborhood was built across a former GOLF COURSE.

This was a fact, which I previously did not know, and which made perfect sense to me, once I saw it: Fairway Lane.

There is a phrase for these kinds of things: *And then, the penny dropped*.

The other part to this story, was that up until this time, I had been unaware that "the penny" *could* drop. I mean, I was one of those kids in the neighborhood who wandered extensively, could be seen cutting across back yards, knew all the shortcuts, either by foot or on bicycle; every house within a mile radius was familiar to me, including the pets, dogs, cats, children.

And then, the penny dropped. My neighborhood was a golf course. And when the penny drops, it comes with a feeling. Like a kind of "wow, I did not know that" feeling.

Part Three

What happens, is that, the first penny drops *accidentally*.

Like when a boy gets his first erection, this usually happens by accident and can be embarrassing if one is not expecting it. What can happen next is that the boy realizes, through his association with other boys, and girls, that such pennies are dropping simultaneously all across the neighborhood.

Then a *second* penny drops, for the young man, that within some of the houses, within the neighborhood, some of *the children* are indoors *playing house*. This offers a fresh depth to *what goes on* within these houses, the things nobody knows, in addition to the proximal shortcuts through back yards, plus the neighbor's pets, dogs, cats, children, fairways.

It's simple to understand (and forgivable) that a boy could get an erection by accident. Perhaps a kind of secret society, comprised of other twelve-year old's, then serves to help this boy understand, that such events happen, not just through accident, but can be CAUSED to happen, under certain circumstances: When you do this, *that* happens. *Shhhh.*

The adults won't explain this. Thus, the child realizes, that there exists a division within the neighborhood: Those who will explain what is going on, and those who won't.

You came into this world on your own and you will leave this world on your own. In the gap of time between, it will be up to you, and whichever inner-circle with which you associate, to figure it all out.

My point is that the first penny drops by accident, which results in about five seconds of amazement and wonder, as everything you thought you knew, shifts. This is called an *epiphany*. An epiphany is an orgasm of *the brain*. Education, in an ideal world, was intended to *cause* such orgasms within the brain, to bring them on, and not discourage them.

Children don't appreciate this, the intended orgasmic-inducing, diabolical nature of education.

Little known is that the extra-ordinary teacher is SUPPOSED to SCREW-UP their lessons. It's the confused STUDENT'S responsibility to *un*screw it up. Also, barely appreciated is that this process will require one's entire lifetime.

We see that within the human BRAIN, there is this thing called one's *intellect*. For the student, who ongoing develops their brain, these individuals are called *intellectually inclined*.

In summary, the epiphany is exactly the same as the boy's erection (in a succession of repetitions). Neither the epiphany nor the erection needs happen by accident, but can be caused.

An intellectual is merely a person who has learned how to give their brain an orgasm.

For us to fully appreciate John Nearly's self-published *Yolita*, certain terms are better defined; the world has allowed certain faked facts to go unnoticed for far too long. If you are still reading, welcome to the secret society of insider-information, an offshoot to society which you have suspected, or known, is beneath the public-forum-veneer since your age of twelve.

It's all those things we've been looking at, but just never saw.

Part Four

Within the category of "intellectual," is likewise a division. The first type, is the FACT-CHECKER, who is not *addicted* to the epiphany. The second type, is the *addict*-FREAK. This type is like a bird gathering little random sticks and pieces of straw, building a nest.

We love the addict-intellectual because from the outside, they appear to have gone mad. They have little bird's nests in their beard or hidden between their breasts, in their hair, scattered on the shelves. They go about in secret, but what they are really doing is collecting pieces of sticks and straw, little tatters of torn fabrics.

Why do they do this? For the hidden joy of it. What's within the joy? Defiance. What is the nature of their defiance, woven through their personal joy? More on that later.

Just to say, that I saw this leaning towards defiance in my own mother. When she drove her children in her car, she drove carefully, obeying the rules. Sometimes, however, she would randomly step on the brakes, causing everybody in the car to lurch forward.

This happened when she saw a POLICE CAR. Except, she wasn't breaking the law. She must have been WANTING to break the law, which is the only explanation I can figure. In other words, *defiance* can sometimes reside within what's otherwise unconscious.

This can go unnoticed unless something external brings it out.

Part Five

One peculiar trait about me as a young adult, was that I knew PRACTICALLY NOTHING.

For example, in college, I was exposed to things which I did not know previously, and one such topic was Virginia Woolf. In high school, we read more-mild authors like Nathaniel Hawthorne: *The Scarlet Letter*. *The Scarlet Letter* was the mild precursor-version of *Lolita*.

Virginia Woolf, that's college level. In college, a student was not required to know much about Virginia Woolf; you need not even learn how to spell her name, just have the ability to recognize the spelling of her name when you saw it.

In other words, I was being educated, while lacking in the appreciation for the nitty-gritty of it, which is, the application of another's artistic expression *to oneself*.

Years later, during the 1980s, an amazing advancement occurred, which was the invention of the video tape and the VCR. This set the average person free from waiting for the local independent movie theater to feature any of the old movie classics, which put all of Hollywood at our fingertips. If you were alive then, recall the miracle of it.

Now I am no intellectual, but I did become more curious about things *after* college, and I do love a good epiphany. So, when I noticed that an old movie had been released to video, *Who's Afraid of Virginia Woolf?*, I instantly recognized the spelling of her name, slapped my two dollars down on the counter, rented it immediately.

Plus, I had adored my mother, and Elizabeth Taylor, who stars in the film, reminded me of my mother, as the kind of beautiful woman who was gracefully aging. Richard Burton, I had less interest in, until I watched him act in *Who's Afraid of Virginia Woolf?*

I put in the video movie anticipating that I was going to learn all about Virginia Woolf. But no, there wasn't much about her through the whole thing.

My parents would not have enjoyed watching this movie; they would have said it was about Hollywood trying to influence people on how to *have a bad marriage*. My mother once said, "There are two types of men. There are talkers and there are doers." This was what my mom said she appreciated about my father, that he was a *doer*.

At this period of my youth, I did not observe my father reading many books, although he did in later years, mostly histories about the Founding Fathers or about the hailing of America's Greatest Generation. When I was a kid, my dad signed-up my brother and me to join the Boy Scouts, which is what doer-dads would do back then.

This is relevant! Because, in Boy Scouts, what do you do? You sit in a group, tell ghost stories around a campfire. Now, *what is* a ghost story? To an idiot-kid, like me, it's a kind of story with a single theme: *Things which lurk*. So, when I read BOOKS, in school, these book-stories were the same to me as ghost stories: Made-up from thin air for the purpose to entertain.

But then, I had an English teacher, who informed her class that LITERATURE is often more COMPLEX. She and I got into an huge argument, after she gave the class an assignment to write an essay about the *themes* within the book, *A Man for All Seasons*. In earnest, I made every attempt to inform her, that *A Man for All Seasons* was merely a STORY, not unlike a ghost story, about a man living in the past and the accidental things which happened to him.

Oh God, she twisted my arm! She forced me to ADMIT that I was wrong, proved me wrong, which I highly resented.

I mean, themes are fine, if you are A TALKER.

All this backstory, just to say, that I was gravely disappointed to discover that this movie I had rented in the 1980s was not A STORY about the person, Virginia Woolf, but about a particular *theme* within Woolf's novels.

The plot, written by Edward Albee, featured two married couples getting together one evening, and what a bad marriage can look like, and the failure of, what should be, a mostly simple ability between two adults to reciprocate, to share in a *give* and a *take*.

But no, the play, and the movie, explored *themes* within Virginia Woolf's novels, which is: banality of existence, social alienation, unmet needs, inappropriate behaviors, and the potential darkness of one's soul, as presented within late 1950s American culture.

This movie, is the unfolding of the *theme* through the characters playing out the details.

I realize that I digress, however, I am rapidly approaching *Lolita*. Lo-li-ta. *Lolita* is another literary example of what a bad marriage looks like, which released to the public in film the same year which *Who's Afraid of Virginia Woolf?* released as a play, 1962.

Keep these things in mind as you read John Nearly's *Yolita*:
The penny drops.
Epiphany.

Nests scattered on shelves within one's subconscious.

Lo-li-ta.
Yo-li-ta.

Part Six

Many of us have heard this quote by Victor Hugo: "Nothing is more powerful than an idea whose time has come."

We hear this phrase and may assume, that there is a *subconscious insert* of two missing words, "to society." Which would fall between the words "powerful" and "than."

"Nothing is more powerful *to society* than ..."

What if we modified this assumption? Extracted the GROUP-THINK. What if, we inserted these three words: "to an individual," falling between "powerful" and "than"?

Nothing is more powerful to an individual than an idea whose time has come.

The difference of meanings is curious.

You could argue, that a person has little influence over their society. Society is too mean, too incongruous, too wayward and vindictive, to be willing to be managed by the various persons attempting to manage it; such that, society swerves *away* from control.

Wasn't this World War II in a nutshell? The motive behind the Allies landing at Normandy Beach? Stop the horrible Nazi *control* of a people within society?

Yet, we can watch, and feel, the impotence of Richard Burton's character, in *Virginia Woolf*, the inability to escape the social control, as we see him *try*. His character relies upon, not himself, but upon his partner, Elizabeth Taylor, and her society, to make the world right.

Later we will notice this same problem within the story of *Lolita*: Where the adult world has devolved *into the moronic*. If you have been following along, this has been my entire point!

Each child turns twelve-years-old in America, and experiences their first epiphany, which is: Nothing is more important than an idea whose time has come.

Part Seven

Please allow me to skip forward to John Nearly, because there are just too many terms to define.

John Nearly is best understood as the character of John Farlow in the film adaptation of Nabokov's novel, *Lolita*. I had also rented this movie back in the 1980s, could not remember the character of John Farlow, so I had to go back and rent it again in 2020.

John Farlow is the husband to Jean, who is the neighbor and best friend to Charlotte Haze, Lolita's mother. John and Jean Farlow's daughter is Mona, Lolita's best friend. Mona appears onscreen for three seconds, however, she comes-up in conversation between the adults several times, so we know who Mona is *to Lolita*.

Mona represents the SECRET SOCIETY of the twelve-to-fourteen-year-olds, as discussed previously, to which Lolita belongs. Most of us have had "a Mona Farlow" from our youth; we can recognize her instantly: The bad girl who is pleasant with the adults.

The movie, *Lolita*, is not about the inner thought-life of a pedophile, Dr. Humbert Humbert.

Lolita is about the secrets we have, or had, and if repetitive, these build on each other, form into a secret-half of ourselves, where we plug into our society, walking both sides of a fence.

Jean Farlow, she's secretive. And Mona Farlow, we easily can infer, she's secretive. The character of John Farlow, the attorney, we can also imply is a MASTER of secretive, *secretive* and skilled at walking the social-fence since his age of twelve.

We meet the FAMILY of the Farlow's in *Lolita* at the town's summer dance-social, which is a formal affair of 1950s culture. Humbert contrasts with the society of this town, because he cannot dance. Thus, Humbert represents, what was referred to in 1950s culture as "the square."

Squares are generally ostracized from "what's really going on." Humbert, clearly would never have been *invited* to such a town event, had he not been brought there through *an insider*. Charlotte Haze, as ignorant as she first appears in the film, we now learn through this dance scene, that she is not as ignorant or awkward as she previously seemed.

We learn more about Charlotte through Jean Farlow, wife of John, mother to Mona, who provocatively comes-on to Humbert during a private conversation at the dance. She informs him that she is "open minded," as is her husband. Humbert, upon hearing this, stands stiff as a deer in headlights, while Jean pulls at his elbow, in effect, to *wake him up*.

She is trying to do him a favor, to wake-up *the square*.

Humbert takes his leave from the adults and the camera follows him, as he sits on the balcony above the dance, then parts the greenery of the plants shielding his view, to watch the children dancing below. Now we know that *squares* can have their own secrets. Meanwhile, the viewer too watches this dance, with the added perspective that the entire room of good citizens, such as John and Jean Farlow, are in the act of making secret deals between each other.

We see the public dance party and can infer that for many, there will be "an after-party."

John Farlow is not just "John Farlow," but represents the BROKER of the after-party life of any normal American small town or metro high society.

Charlotte Haze is similarly, actively involved in social choreography, and we see this in the scene following the dance of her with Humbert, finally alone together, at *their* after-party. She has "slipped into something more comfortable," pre-prepared a small banquet, pre-selected the music, premeditated her own kind of dance-floor scene, including champagne, properly chilled.

Humbert gets cornered by Charlotte Hayes
as Lolita watches from the staircase.

The Humbert we saw earlier as the observer-square, his bluff is being called by Charlotte. Yet he counters her every move, just as skillfully, because he's no dummy.

His squareness is his ACT.

We also see this as Humbert is SAVED by Lolita, who has returned home early from the afterparty being given at the Farlow's. This serves to SHATTER THE FAÇADE, brings relief to the viewer, that these three characters, suddenly together again, are no longer pretending to be what they are not.

Charlotte really does want to scream, weep, feel sorry for herself. Lolita really does enjoy torturing her mother. Humbert really does want to make the perfect sandwich for Lolita before she goes off to bed.

Here is what's key to notice: Lolita has been *sitting there* watching Humbert with Charlotte BEFORE they notice her. This is no ACCIDENT. The tables have been TURNED. We had watched the dance through Humbert's eyes; now we observe the dance through Lolita's eyes.

Through Lolita's eyes, comes clarity. Now who's square? Charlotte Haze is square. John and Jean and Mona are square. The whole town, with all of its secrets together, is square, in *contrast* to Humbert, as we see him resist Charlotte, through the eyes of Lolita.

Undercurrents are fine as long as they are sanctioned. What happens when two people meet, form their own private undercurrent, which is not sanctioned? And this is what the entire rest of the film, *Lolita*, explores. Undercurrents which *defy* undercurrents.

Except for one teeny, tiny glitch in the matrix.

Part Eight

We must broaden the lens, to grasp this glitch in the matrix.

Expand our scope to include Washington DC at this same time period, 1952.

This societal dance in Small Town, New Hampshire, thematically represents ALL of America, the multi-layers of what's going on, and what's *really* going on. For that, we should know that General Dwight D. Eisenhower simultaneously, in real life 1952, is in the process of being elected America's 34th president.

What we cannot see, are two men behind the political scenes, intimately involved in getting General Dwight D. Eisenhower elected as president of the United States, who are brother attorneys, Allen and John Foster Dulles. They are the 1952 MASTERS of WHAT'S SECRETIVE.

The Dulles brothers are the real-life characters making things happen, who are *represented* by the attorney and swinger, John Farlow, in the film, *Lolita*.

Dwight D. Eisenhower represents THE SQUARE, like Humbert, who has his own secrets, kept private and away from scrutiny.

And yes, Allen and John are the same Dulles, for which the International Airport in Washington DC is still named. We will see this more clearly later, that the Dulles' name represents *something else*: What the public sees, versus what is REALLY going on. The politics which the public sees, and what is really going on. The "John and Jean Farlow" characters who the moviegoer sees, and what is really going on in the town, off-camera.

Under the new Eisenhower administration, John Foster Dulles will be named Secretary of State. Allen Dulles will be named as Director of the C IA, yes, in real-life action figures.

And President John F. Kennedy, ironically, will have the privilege of naming this DC airport: *Dulles*.

Why? Kennedy wanted to name it *Chantilly*, so why *Dulles*? His arm was twisted, in the same way that Jean Farlow was attempting to twist the arm of Humbert Humbert. "You know what I mean," she was saying, while tugging.

Which twisting? Former President Eisenhower's twisting of Kennedy's arm in 1961, while Allen Dulles, Director of the CIA, was twisting Eisenhower's arm. And there we have it: *Dulles International Airport*, per the next *new* president, Kennedy.

Appears quite *normal*, to me. How about to you? *Dulles* Airport? Just a name?

A shark will bump its prey to test for the compliance to be eaten. In the case of naming this airport, Kennedy proved himself compliant. Later, when he refused to comply, this caught Allen Dulles, Director of the C IA, by surprise. Dulles had bumped into his prey, which seemed compliant, but now this prey escaped; Kennedy suddenly turned non-compliant.

No, Mr. Kennedy will not escape Allen Dulles for a second time.

Kennedy with Allen Dulles

What I mean is, there was more going on in America in 1952, and in 1962, than meets the eye. We see this also in literature, in *Who's Afraid of Virginia Woolf?* And in *Lolita*.

This is the history from which we Americans originate, the World Wars and the post-war society rolled into today's (children become parents) timeline.

The Washington DC formal dances, bow ties, chiffon, whispers, nods, winks, light kicks under the table, the this and the that's, what's taught about America through education, and what's not. The secret affairs of the fictional John Farlow's, the many roles of the fictional American wives in 1952, their children's roles, the Lolita's and the Mona's coming of age all across America.

Part Nine

Let's dig under it, shall we? Regarding something which I randomly stumbled upon. A self-published and obscure memoir, *Yolita*, by a John Nearly. In his memoir, he claims to be the real-life person upon which the fictional character, John Farlow, was based.

His memoir you can read right here FOR YOURSELF. Please do not take my word on it! "Truth is stranger than fiction," was coined by somebody else, not me. If you asked my opinion on Thumbert and John Nearly, I think that both of them were touched by madness. I'd even wonder if they hadn't experimented with LSD together while in California.

My guess, is that they were the sort of two friends who "egged each other into things," quite possibly the first two original, tall-tale international conspiracy theorists.

Anyway, it is clearly true that Vladimir Nabokov wrote *Lolita*, as fiction. After learning of John Nearly, whether he had served as inspiration for Nabokov's character of John Farlow, I did a little research into it; was the real John Nearly somehow connected to Nabokov?

What I learned comes from a *New Yorker* article titled, "The Salacious Non-Mystery of 'The Real Lolita,'" September 17, 2018. The origins of *Lolita* may date back to 1948, when a man named Frank La Salle posed as an F BI agent, commanded an eleven-year-old girl, Sally Horner, to come with him. As detailed in *The New Yorker*, "Like Humbert Humbert, the protagonist of the novel *Lolita*, La Salle concealed his predations by posing as his victim's father."

A nonfiction book released in 2018, titled, *The Real Lolita*, by Sarah Weinman, in which she pulls back the veil on a kidnapping that made national news in 1952, perhaps inspired Nabokov to write *Lolita*. Again, I wondered, if Sally Horner was the original Lolita, was

John Nearly the original John Farlow, as Nearly claimed to be in his book, *Yolita*, dating to 1962?

In 2019, the story continues, which in November of that year, I stumbled across perhaps the last copy on the planet of John Nearly's personal memoir. What struck me immediately was the subtitle: *The Lectures of Thumbert Thumbert*. Was there some sort of TIE between *Yolita* with *Lolita,* and Thumbert with Humbert? I had to know.

According to John Nearly, Humbert Humbert's character was based upon, NOT any kind of kidnapping in 1948, but on something else. And only Nabokov, and about five other individuals knew about it, including John Nearly. Secretive, behind the scenes stuff we could not know.

Until now.

I apologize, but once again, there is a *backstory* to all of this.

Part Ten

December 7, 1941, Japan bombed Pearl Harbor.

Who was the president of America at this time? Franklin D. Roosevelt. One of the most famous military colonels at this juncture in 1941 was a man named William Donovan, famous partly for his bravery as a soldier during WWI, portrayed in a popular film released in 1940, *The Fighting 69th*, starring James Cagney.

Pay attention to the events: Roosevelt blundered, Japan bombs Hawaii, a publicly famous military colonel from WWI named Donovan comes to the rescue.

After Pearl Harbor, Donovan went to Roosevelt, to discuss how to avoid such tragic blunders. Colonel Donovan discovered that there were twelve different intelligence agencies reporting to the president, including every branch of the military. In 1942, Donovan offered to consolidate such intelligence reporting into one CENTRALIZING agency, to be named The Office of Strategic Services (OSS), which five years later became the C entral I ntelligence A gency.

A sad thing happened in April, 1945, which was the death of Roosevelt, which was doubly-sad for William Donovan, because the successor to FDR was Harry Truman. Truman felt threatened by Bill Donovan, because in many ways, Donovan was vastly more popular with the voting public. At this time, there was an F BI, as we all know, headed by J. Edgar Hoover, who was *also* jealous of William Donovan, because Hoover believed that HE should head a *combined* agency of the F BI and the OSS, with the popular (now General) Donovan connected to *none* of it.

William Donovan had the misfortune of being too patriotic, brave, and honest, which are dangerous qualities to men like Truman and J. Edgar Hoover.

General Donovan (1883-1959)

When J. Edgar Hoover learned that Donovan had petitioned Roosevelt, and then Truman, to launch a broader kind of OSS following WWII, Hoover stepped-in to block it. He released to his press contacts that William Donovan was attempting to form "an American version" of the Nazi Gestapo right here in the U.S. Hoover also spread a rumor that Donovan was having a marital affair with his daughter-in-law, and later, that Donovan had syphilis. This news coverage gave Truman the necessary out, to disband the OSS, along with Donovan's leadership of it, in 1945.

Most Americans today have never heard of the OSS, nor of William Donovan, but at the time of its disbanding, it had 13,000 personnel, with 750,000 pages in its personnel files. This was no small accomplishment to occur within a few short years, then disbanded within ten days by Harry Truman.

According to John Nearly, *he* served in the OSS, and for several months in 1944, was as an aide to the then Brigadier General Donovan. In 1947, Truman reauthorized the work of the OSS, *without* Donovan, an organization which came to be known as the C IA.

In 1953, Allen Dulles became its first civilian director and went on to serve until 1961, then fired by President Kennedy after the Bay of Pigs fiasco in Cuba.

Nearly was brought back to work in Intelligence in 1948, whereupon he claims to have met a man named Herbert Thunberg, in post-war Berlin. Dr. Herbert Thunberg, of Russian birth, was living in Nuremberg through most of WWII. Thunberg had been a professor of French literature and an outsider to the Nazi Party, while he also possessed information valuable to the American and British governments.

This backstory might be summed up: Both Thunberg and Nearly had connections to very high levels of U.S. authority and intelligence, while SERVING at the lower levels.

Thunberg received training in London, then returned to Berlin, where he was directly recruited by Allen Dulles, himself. Nearly was given the task of communicating between a C IA office in Chicago and the office in Berlin, to assure that Thunberg emigrated to the U.S. in good order.

Nearly claims that he was assigned to be Thunberg's "handler," otherwise known as his case officer. It was in this capacity that Nearly assisted Thunberg to move to Des Moines, Iowa, in 1950 to help monitor U.S. magazine distribution facilities undercover as a French literature professor at Drake University.

Nearly also claims that through a clerical error in Berlin, Herbert Thunberg's name was typed as a Dr. Thumbert Thumbert; I know, you can't make this up.

You may be wondering, how do *I* know any of this?

How does one random suburban-neighborhood kid, such as myself, who claims that he doesn't know *anything*, suddenly know so much? William Donovan. Harry Truman. Herbert Thunberg. John Nearly. Allen Dulles. *Lolita.* Virginia Woolf. How to spell her name. Etcetera.

I'll get to that, if you will just be patient.

Part Eleven

My father's younger brother, my Uncle Mike, served in the Marines 1964 to 1966 during the Vietnam War. While there, he met his best friend for the rest of his life, a man named Fred. Fred and his wife later resided in Arlington, Virginia. In 1985, the house next-door to Fred was selling at a price well-below market value. Fred contacted my Uncle Mike regarding this house for sale, then from 1985 till 2020, Fred and my uncle continued their friendship as next-door neighbors until Fred's passing.

My father and mother had retired to South Carolina. In 2019, my parents were going to drive to visit my Uncle Mike and my Aunt Mae. Because the drive to Virginia would be long for my parents, now in their eighties, I offered to drive to South Carolina myself, then help them drive to visit my aunt and uncle for two days in Virginia, then back again.

Over the years, my parents had become casual acquaintances with Fred and his wife, also named May, except spelled with a Y. I had never heard of them, myself. Fred was in poor health in 2019; my uncle suggested that he and my father might pay him a quick visit to cheer him up. I had nothing better to do, so I tagged along.

I also heard my aunt tell my mother, in hushed tones, that Fred was not just an English language teacher, but that he had served with the C IA for over thirty years.

Fred greeted us, but was wheelchair bound, in the early stages of the disease, ALS. The four of us sat in the living room, a very lovely house, all around. The topic turned to the Marines and to Vietnam, when Fred asked if *I* wouldn't mind running upstairs to grab a photo off the wall, of Uncle Mike and Fred in Saigon, 1965.

When I reached the top of the stairs, there was an open room, a library of sorts, filled with shelves of books, little statues, trophies, and sculptures, framed photos of people also on the shelves and on every wall. I was interested in the books, for either Fred was well-read or else a fine book collector. I saw the photo of Fred with my uncle in 1965, just as my eyes caught the words on the spine of a book: *Yolita – The Lectures of Thumbert Thumbert.*

Fred called from the living room, "How's it going there, Scott? Have you found the photo?"

I called back, "Yes, I'm just admiring your book collection!"

Fred replied, "Yes, there are quite a few books up there."

I quickly pulled *Yolita* from the shelf, flipped through it, saw some photos of a young woman in a bathing suit, started back down the stairs carrying this book and the framed photo. I wanted to ask Fred about the book, but then, I thought it improper, perhaps to have pulled-it off the shelf, so I set it on a little side table in the hallway, intended to return it, when I returned the photo.

However, Fred never asked me to put the framed photo back. As we were leaving, Fred, Uncle Mike, and my father, were engaged in conversation, going out another way from where I had laid the book. I didn't mean to take it, I just did, slipped it under my jacket.

Upon returning home, I unpacked my suitcase, took out this book, *Yolita*, threw it onto a stacked pile of old mail I had yet to open. And there it sat for a year, on top of that mail, and more junk mail, which had been thrown on top of *Yolita*.

In 2020, that very strange year when people were staying at home, I decided to de-junk. That's when I again stumbled across, and read through, this very bizarre book, *Yolita*. The author, John Nearly, self-published it in early 1963 (which I have republished here).

I conducted an internet search, turned-up an interesting connection. "John Nearly" and "Yolita" linked to a declassified list of items found in the garage of a Michael and Ruth Paine on November 23, 1963. This was the Dallas home where Lee Harvey Oswald and his wife, Marina, were living at the time of the Kennedy assassination. It was listed as "a box of 24 books" with the title, *Yolita, The Lectures of Thumbert Thumbert.*

The box went into the custody of the D allas p olice. Also listed was another box containing lesbian pornographic films, which I learned later belonged to Ruth Paine, and the films were returned to her, but not the box of 24 books.

I am guessing, that *one* of the 24 book copies, circulated the offices of the C IA in McLean, Virginia, and somehow ended-up in Fred's office. From there, to his home library, where it likely sat for thirty, forty years, before I picked it up, and I suppose, I stole it.

Fred passed-away three months after our visit, and my Uncle Mike passed last year, so what I REALLY did was to SAVE a book that would have ended-up in the trash heap of history. Deep down I felt this on the day I had stolen the book; I'm not a *thief*, just a preservationist.

Part Twelve

However, that's not the end of the story, how I came into the possession of *Yolita*.

How did a Thumbert become a HUMBERT?

This is all explained in *Yolita*, if you are inclined to read it.

Yolita with her mother, Charmin Hayes
Des Moines, 1949

Recall that John Nearly was Thumbert's Intelligence Agency HANDLER.

There were high expectations within the Intelligence Agency, that Thumbert was an extraordinary asset. Thumbert *was* a French literary professor, yes, but he was also a self-taught expert in rocket propulsion, sent on a mission to gather information on Jack Parsons, the former brilliant partner in the Jet Propulsion Lab.

Thumbert indeed, married a widower, Charmin Hayes, who had a daughter, Yolita. After the marriage, Charmin was sent to Paris for six months, leaving Yolita in Thumbert's care, with full assurances that the Nearly family would also be looking after her through her final year in high school, because Yolita was sixteen going on seventeen, not age fourteen, certainly not *twelve*.

Thumbert indeed, brought Yolita with him on his long road trips to California.

But then, something turned sour, after Jack Parsons died in a lab explosion, June 17, 1952. Thumbert was arrested in July, charged under the Mann Act for "transporting a woman across state lines." And Nearly, still Thumbert's handler, visited him several times in jail.

Thumbert indeed, kept a journal, and had formed his notes into a memoir, which he was completing in jail. His memoir was also titled *Yolita*, with no subtitle. I believe that Nearly had read the manuscript, which was smuggled-out from Thumbert's jail cell.

Nearly reported all of this to his superiors, however, it was also known that Thumbert had more than one copy, with additional visitors while in jail, including Yolita. Apparently, this manuscript was not flattering to U.S. Intelligence Services nor to its director, Allen Dulles. The problem was that Thumbert's *Yolita* manuscript could have turned up anywhere, including at some obscure, dark-themed publisher, then made PUBLIC.

The C IA could take no risks. For one, recall that in 1952, the Cold War was in fever pitch.

Thumbert did not survive in jail, and his manuscript, *Yolita*, disappeared.

In 1955, John Nearly's supervising officer provided him a copy of Vladimir Nabokov's *Lolita*, written in French. As Thumbert's former handler, Nearly was asked to file a report on this French book, *Lolita*.

Apparently, Nearly was one of two people still alive in 1955, who knew who Thumbert Thumbert really was, and perhaps the *only* person still alive, who had read Thumbert's manuscript, *Yolita*.

Nearly reported to his superiors that *Lolita* hit very *close to the mark*. Naturally, this was what they wanted to hear, that John Nearly could be trusted to remain QUIET.

However, over the course of their three-year friendship, Thumbert had gotten-to Nearly, twisted his mind, so to speak.

Apparently, Nearly was never married to Jean; this was a cover. Moana was actually Jean's daughter through a previous marriage. Thumbert and Nearly spent a fair number of evenings together, which was mostly Dr. Thumbert musing, or lecturing, off the top of his head.

According to Nearly, the Agency needed to DISCREDIT Thumbert, in the event that his manuscript, *Yolita*, could appear from nowhere in book form, so an outside author was brought in, Vladimir Nabokov, to *paint* the actual C IA asset, Thumbert, as the pedophile, Humbert.

This happens all the time! It happened to General William Donovan, and if it happened to him, it could happen to anybody.

This adaptation was super easy: Nearly became Farlow, Thumbert became Humbert, Charmin became Charlotte, Moana became Mona, and Yolita became Lolita. They wanted the ghost writer to have a Russian name, to be written from the mind of *a Russian*, which served a dual purpose, that the story of *Lolita* came from a Russian novelist; *never would a true-blue American* be a pedophile.

According to John Nearly, the fake character of Humbert *never violated* the fake character of Lolita.

The *real* Thumbert adored the *real* Yolita, this is true, while he only had sought to protect her from the darker forces of American society, and now we know: He failed.

Part Thirteen

The publishing of Nabokov's *Lolita* in September, 1955, in France, lit a fuse which caused a worldwide readership explosion, like a phenomenon we call today *going viral*. Graham Greene, in the London *Sunday Times*, called it one of the three best books of 1955. While John Gordon, with the London *Sunday Express*, called it "the filthiest book I have ever read" and "sheer unrestrained pornography."

This novel came to be one of the best-sellers of ALL TIME with over 50 million copies sold.

Yes, Vladimir Nabokov wrote *Lolita*. Except WHY he wrote it, this freak anomaly of a storytelling confessional, *Lolita*, has been hidden from us, intentionally and subversively.

How *Lolita* came into print was through a series of perfect accidents. And it is likewise through accident, that you now hold this truthful version of *Yolita* in your hands, as it came to me, just as *accidental* as anything ever was.

Then, the adaptation of Humbert's original, was *further* adapted by Hollywood, released to the general public in 1962. In this film version, we are introduced to the friends of Charlotte Haze, Jean and John Farlow, intimately connected to the story from beginning to end. Understand that nobody could know then, what I know now.

Thus, between 1952 to 1962, time apparently marched further from the truth.

With the release of *Lolita*, the film, apparently John Nearly watched it, had had *enough*.

He would set the record straight. Thus, <u>Version One</u>, *Yolita*, was a confessional penned by "Dr. Thumbert," nonfiction, 1953, lost.

<u>Version Two</u>, *Lolita*, the adaptation to Thumbert's *Yolita*, penned by Vladimir Nabokov, fiction, 1955, bestseller.

<u>Version Three</u>, *Yolita: The Lectures of Thumbert Thumbert*, by John Nearly, nonfiction, 1963; lost, one remaining copy found, you are holding it in your hands.

That's it, in a nutshell.

Part Fourteen

Back in 1955, pornography was not the same, as what it is today. I mean, it was exactly the same *in nature* as it is today, just more limited in *distribution*. Like *pornography* wasn't as readily available to the AVERAGE TEEN, who is given their first Smart phone, as it is today. Low estimates state that 4 percent of all internet websites are pornographic in nature, with a possible high of 37 percent.

We'd want to know, why this crazy swing in pornography *estimates* (between 4 to 37%)? Because there are at least 4.5 billion websites indexed by search engines (coincidentally the generally accepted number of years which the planet Earth has existed). Meanwhile, there is a whole another Internet called the "Deep Web," which a Google search does not penetrate (Google skims merely 4 percent of what's out there).

At minimum (4%), the number of sex acts captured on film, given twenty to one-hundred "filmed sex acts" per website, that's roughly 4.5 billion naked people filmed in the act, mostly with their own permission, and we want to know, who *are* these people? *You*?

And who are their *viewers*? Because the sheer numbers are pointing us to the fact that every adult male on the planet is watching porn, including every gender-type, with some straight females hidden in the mix, so that does not leave many, remaining eligible, non-porn-watchers.

I won't belabor the point, but collectively, the quantity of porn available on the deep web, the dark web, and up to 37 percent of the other 4.5 billion websites, comprises our social subconscious or "what's running through the collective adult-mind" on a daily basis.

How is it that SEX could SHOCK *any* of us?

Yolita visiting Parsons (without Thumbert)
Taken in California, 1952
Photos enhanced in 2024 from Nearly's book using AI.

Thus *Lolita*, published in 1955, in France, if pornographic, represents the very tip of an inverted pyramid illustrating the statistics of what was, and what was to become, the world as we know it today (highly pornographic), with or without a fictional work such as *Lolita*.

Apparently, the original draft was written by Dr. Thumbert (Dr. Herbert Thunberg), and then adapted by Vladimir Nabokov through various connections with various motivations.

That is my summary of all I know about any of it.

Part Fifteen

This story, *Yolita*, provides us no psychiatric forward, because the author, John Nearly, self-published this account in the spring of 1963, had one-hundred paperback books printed, sent copies to various friends and acquaintances, according to the author's son, shortly before John Nearly's death, June 17, 1963, at age 55, from the rapid onset of pancreatic cancer.

Not much else is known about the backstory regarding the writing of *Yolita, The Lectures of Thumbert Thumbert*, aside from the content of the book itself. That is, until November, 1963, when the garage of a certain Michael and Ruth Paine was searched by the D allas p olice.

Now I had found John Nearly's son online, still living in Chicago, began an email correspondence. I wanted to know about the PHOTOS contained in *Yolita*. With AI technology, I was able to salvage most of them for republication. I was told that Nearly had discovered the photos in Thumbert's apartment, after jailed, as Thumbert constantly documented everything.

Some of the photographs Thumbert had taken from the Hayes household library. Others were shot during Yolita's visits with Jack Parsons in California. The story of Yolita represents the story of her generation, so I'd suppose that the pictures tell a generational story, as well.

I *do* know this, that to be human, is to appreciate that other humans are naked beneath their clothes, a realization, which most often occurs at a time when we are young, alone, and by ourselves. And have you noticed? That from this very beginning, of time, I mean, *somebody* must take the blame.

I'd blame Adam. Who would you blame?

Scott Wright Webb
January 14, 2024
Nashville, Tennessee

YOLITA

The Lectures of Thumbert Thumbert

By John B. Nearly

Each of us is all the sums he has not counted: subtract us into nakedness and night again, and you shall see begin in Crete four thousand years ago the love that ended yesterday in Texas.

The seed of our destruction will blossom in the desert, the alexin of our cure grows by a mountain rock, and our lives are haunted by a Georgia slattern, because a London cutpurse went unhung. Each moment is the fruit of forty thousand years. The minute-winning days, like flies, buzz home to death, and every moment is a window on all time.

--Thomas Wolfe, *Look Homeward, Angel*

Chapter 1

When Thumbert's manuscript, renamed *Lolita,* published in 1955 and ghost-written by Vladimir Nabokov, it was my job to read through it, which was impossible, because I could not read French. Thus, a translator was provided by the Agency, and I knew from the first paragraph, that this task set before me was a test. They wanted to know whether I'd *talk.*

Straight away, and I did not delay, I confirmed each and every detail, knowing fully of the FARCE that it was. You would need to appreciate how the Agency works, i.e., by compartmentalization, for example, that in the building of the first atomic bomb, one hand could not know what the other was doing.

It's like that parable of the blind men feeling parts of an elephant. One man feels the tail, says it's a rope, another feels the ear, says it's a fan, etc.

I'd have to say, that for many years, I was precisely so blind, and fairly certain of a certain truth, and then, you know, your eyes are one day opened as the scales fall off.

And what do you do about it? You shut up about it!

You say, "Yes, indeed, it's a rope."

This is the most basic lesson. Never let ANYONE KNOW if your eyes have once been opened.

Chapter 2

I first met Dr. Thumbert Thumbert after the war, and this was in Europe, Germany to be precise, 1948. He was some kind of captured "war criminal," and as part of Operation Paperclip, he was to be brought to the United States to work in the new Intelligence Services. He had no paperwork backing his identity, so I brought him to the military base in Berlin and was standing right there when the idiot-kid in uniform was taking down his information.

"Name?"

"Herbert Thunberg."

Now I knew this was a fake, "Herbert Thunberg," certainly an alias, and my job as a representative of the U.S. government, was to push it all through, sign documents, etc. It was two years later that this gentleman eventually emigrated to the U.S., following extensive training in London, and I was called upon to meet him at the airport to settle him into his new life in the Free World and democracy, etc.

My agenda that day in Chicago was to meet a certain Thumbert Thumbert at the airport, and I was told that this was the same person I had met in Berlin, whereupon he explained it to me himself, once I recognized his face. An unfortunate clerical error had been made in the typing of his paperwork in Berlin and could not be changed.

A *twist of fate* turned a *Herbert Thunberg* into a Thumbert Thumbert.

"Well, if it cannot be changed," I said while slapping him on the back, "Heil Hitler!"

Chapter 3

I was based out of Chicago, unmarried, just turned 29. I had a 6-year-old son who lived with his mother, and her parents, in Arlington Heights, and it's a long story, but I myself lived in Oak Park, took the train to work in the Downtown Loop.

Jean Dobrowski worked in another department, but in the same building as I did, age 33, also a parent to a daughter, Moana, age fourteen.

Long story short, Jean and I met on the train, and soon, we were living together, the three of us, circa 1950, John, Jean, and Moana. Under these circumstances, our supervisors told us that Jean and I were being sent to Des Moines on a short-term mission, together. Our cover was that we were "married," and of course, living together. As you may have guessed by now, we were the Nearly's.

Jean was placed as assistant to the president of Drake College, while I was to watch-for/monitor any subversive activity in U.S. magazine distribution, as Des Moines is famously centrally located within the States, while our other mission was to be a kind of "handler" of this new recruit, Thumbert Thumbert.

This was a temporary assignment until Dr. Thumbert could be placed more permanently, and as far as I know, he never ONCE set foot in the great state of New Hampshire.

And to set the stage, this was the very tip of an iceberg, which came to be what I call LIES.

And here's the question: *Who's* lies?

Photo I snapped of Yolita with Moana and my mother.
Des Moines, September, 1950

Chapter 4

One thing, just to point out, and the reader will realize, as it took me a bit more time to realize, that Thumbert's memoir, *Yolita*, was NOT about "incest," and NOT about human trafficking, nor pedophilia, but it was about, how quickly *the human mind* can calculate and spit out lies.

I'll offer one such example, within the very first lines, Chapter One of Nabokov's book.

"Lolita, light of my life, fire of my loins. My sin, my soul."

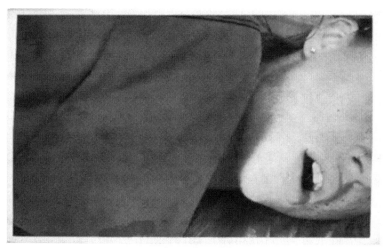

Yolita sleeping
Photo taken by Thumbert while on the road, 1952

No, think about it! "Humbert" is supposed to be a GROWN MAN of 37 years, a German, a Russian, an intensely well-read man of letters, who has absolutely NOTHING in common with a twelve-year-old girl, and *this* is his HINDSIGHT, of his supposed-memoir?

"LIGHT OF MY LIFE?" Yolita? Hilarious.

And I was there, and none of this could be further from the truth.

Not the words of the Thumbert I knew, who was actually 40.

Think about it! In the exact same fashion in which Humbert constantly lied to Lolita, (and she to him), Nabokov is lying to the reader. And I wish you could have seen the expression on my French translator's face when she first read those first lines to me and I laughed out loud.

My sin, my soul.

I howled.

It was all *making sense*.

Thumbert's sins. I mean, this was *invented*, Humbert's sins, as *Thumbert's* sins.

Biblical confession was not in Thumbert's vocabulary, either, and I would know, having listened to every one of his lectures.

Chapter 5

Nabokov's Humbert tells us directly in his manuscript that he is being observed, that he is writing "while in prison."

Metaphorically, yes! This entire planet is their prison! And they, the prison's guards.

This is the one truth we can count on. Thumbert had an *editor*. And with one stroke of the keyboard, Thumbert becomes Humbert. What did *they* edit out? And what did they edit *in*?

If you hadn't been there, as I had been, you wouldn't know, could you? And then I am telling you plain: This is the brilliance of the storyteller. You are being lied to, exactly as the characters lie to each other in *Lolita*, and we BELIEVE this confessor is Humbert, and I'm telling you, it wasn't him telling you his story in Nabokov's *Lolita*.

Chapter 6

Then "literary critics" explain "the novel," all across America, that "the brilliance of the work" is that the reader is made "sympathetic to a pedophile." No, no, NO!

The "brilliance" is that "literary criticism" is generally full of shit.

Literary criticism is part of the *propaganda* narrative.

The deeper issue is that there's no money in the truth.

Take me, for example, and *my* own memoir: *Yolita.* I'll likely print twenty copies and be done with it! The truth always is paid-for from one's own pocket, just a rule of thumb.

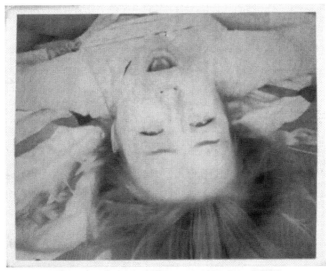

Photo taken by Charmin Hayes, 1949
On the back of the photo was written,
"Typical morning telling Yo to wake-up
(she was late again for school)."
"I am not my daughter's keeper!"

Chapter 7

Another truth in the novel is that the young Thumbert, back in his younger days of Annabella relations, is that she wanted someday to be a nurse, and Thumbert wrote that he wanted to be *what*? A SPY!

I can vouch for the truth of this.

Think about it! Where does H̲umbert get his money?! Recall, he tells L̲olita that they can leave their town IMMEDIATELY, and she asks him, "What about your *job*?"

He explains that this is, but a mere triviality: "He's walking-out on his teaching job" in the middle of a semester? Is this credible? And that, his new job will be that he will "write essays" for hire?

Do we believe this nonsense?

That they will be traveling across the country, staying in hotels nightly, eating every meal out? No, Thumbert has *other means*. He's lying to L̲olita, and he's lying to you, the reader.

He's a freaking Operation Paperclip, U.S. government sanctioned, government funded, government edited, SPY. It says it right there in Nabokov's book: He wants to be a spy.

I alone, am left to separate, fact from fiction.

Photo by Charmin Hayes, summer, 1950
"Junior counselors with camp directors."

Chapter 8

And what of Annabella? Do we, the readers, swallow this throb of a fairytale, that "Lolita" is the result of a groping he once did with Annabella, from back in Europe as Humbert was an adolescent? And then tragically, Annabella died, and deep within his Freudian psyche, this must be replayed over and over again to be *resolved* through pedophilia?

So Humbert can be fully "a man" now?

And no mention is made by the critics, that this is hardly credible, the entire Nabokov memoir, if this one part was entirely falsified: Humbert's Freudian psyche underpinning a pedophile.

Think about it! If you are a man now, and still groping children, is this the best you can *invent*? That you *never recovered* from that flame you had had from the fourth grade?

And if you are a woman, are you buying this form of *excuse* from a self-confessed pedophile?

And let's look at this Humbert character himself. On one level, he has no patience for stupidity, this we know. So, yes, no, this Annabella story: Could an intelligent, self-aware Humbert even write of it? And his *excuse*? No, this is *a clear clue*, dear reader, he didn't, and I mean, YOU know it.

Chapter 9

Now I am going to tell you what really happened: Because I was *there*.

We all know Nabokov's story as we were told: Pedophile accidentally meets young girl, he marries her mother to be close to young girl, abuses mother in every manner which a husband could, even considering murder; circumstances throw "pedophile" and girl together. Pedophile does more bad things, girl does bad things, she runs away. This murderous tendency returns, man must murder, repeating once again "doing another bad thing" to another fellow human-being, to find *his own* healing.

The READER rides Nabokov's absurdist rollercoaster. Millions of copies of this fun-ride sell.

Post-war America, 1950s repression/lies-all-lies, fake your way through, is the story's backdrop.

And, as explained in the Forward to LOLITA, *pedophiliacs* comprise somewhere "between ten to fifteen percent" of the general population, so this story is hardly unique, and therefore completely *believable*. Because we believe everything we are told. Did I get it right?

What comes next herewith, is first Thumbert's *real* story, and secondly, I'll briefly reframe the post-war America 1950s repression/lies-all-lies backdrop. And now, like the Apostle Paul, I write this in my own hand to prove a certain validity. This is *me*, John Nearly, and no other.

Chapter 10

First of all, *Thumbert* was coincidentally, an average-sized man who happened to have two enormous and out-of-proportion thumbs. This explains how the name "Herbert Thunberg" somehow came to be typed on the passport paperwork as Thumbert Thumbert, whether intentional, or perfectly accidental, I'm not sure which.

Apparently, such features as appendages on a man can appear attractive to the opposite sex and sometimes just as attractive to the same sex. However, this overgrowth did not apply to any other appendages of his human body.

I realize that this detail might be highly personal, however, with Thumbert passing in 1953, I see no harm in relaying a certain confession, made to me by this same man, while we sat in a Hamburg bar, after consuming several local lagers.

He described, that women were instantly attracted to him, while he had *no staying power*, and this he attributed to his *being a poet*, a kind of premature ecstasy of the mind, and body, from the simplest of stimulations. He confessed that if even a butterfly were to alight upon his finger, he could instantly "ejaculate in his pants."

This was his peculiar curse, he said, stating that, to get out of more *romantic situations*, he found, that claiming to have *a toothache* was the perfect excuse to make his exit, to protect his secret, that even a woman removing a sock in his presence was more than he could take.

And I know, for a fact, that this world-renown "pedophile," never *once* had sex with a twelve or even a fourteen-year-old, but how many times he came in his own pants, I couldn't say, might have been daily. At least, once a week, I'd guess, for he was a sensitive type.

Yolita, 1951, taken by Charmin Hayes
Written on back: "Stayed-up all night
sewing Yo's costume for the school play."

Chapter 11

I was there that day when Thumbert first saw Yolita, in real life, not this Humbert tale of first laying eyes on *Lo*-li-ta.

For reasons known only to the editors, *I* was written-out.

But it was *I*, who met Thumbert, at Midway Airport in Chicago, and since Jean, and he, were both starting work at Drake, the three of us were driving to Des Moines together. Jean and I were already resettled there, as mentioned, as the Nearly's, just three weeks earlier.

Our new home was three doors down from one, Charmin Hayes, and Thumbert's living accommodations had *already been* settled, and it was my job to make sure this happened at the Hayes house.

Harold Hayes, Charmin's dead husband, dearly departed seven years prior, was NOT in the insurance business, as was *her* impression, but was a gun-runner for secret U.S. operations in Central America 1925 to 1943, when he was killed in a small plane crash outside Guatemala City. Harold Hayes, according to the Agency, was the biggest and best liar of them all, and due to be promoted as station chief at the time of his untimely death.

Rumors within the Agency were that Harold Hayes knew too much and was beginning to crack.

Gone for weeks at a time, Mr. Hayes was away "on business" when Charmin became pregnant with Yolita, and it was everything she could do to give him the impression that Yolita was his, which resulted in added-friction in the raising of young Yolita, prior to Charmin's husband's death.

And then he died, ending a relatively bad marriage; the designation "of sainthood" applied by Charmin to Harold *after* he was dearly departed.

It was *I* who brought Thumbert to the Hayes home, all prearranged; there was no "choice" in the matter, and this was at night, for it was quite late when we arrived, and Charmin and Yolita were in a screaming match, which we could hear quite clearly from the driveway. Thumbert raised a brow to me as we rang the doorbell, and as the door opened, following a long delay, we did see the back of Yolita, yes, running up the stairs to her bedroom.

This other story of Yolita (Lolita) sunning herself on the back lawn as Thumbert first laid eyes upon her, all pure embellishment and somebody else's editorial license, no question. I was there.

The only other part of the story, was that Charmin Hayes served us both a generous slice of her cherry pie. Again, quite late. Then Thumbert developed a toothache, and rather abruptly, went off to settle himself in his room.

Chapter 12

The details of Thumbert's childhood and upbringing in Russia are but a fog to me because Thumbert was mostly private in all his dealings. He did speak of his year in London, and later in Berlin, through the rise of Nazism to the end of the War. He did confess, in *his* version of *Yolita*, that from a young age, he dreamed of being A SPY.

I cannot tell you for whom he spied, whether for the British or for the Germans; certainly he had no love for the Bolsheviks. If he had sided with Germany during the War, I would assume it was due to his despising the communists.

I do know for a fact, that Thumbert was present in Switzerland in 1944, that *he* preferred that Germany surrender to *the Western Allies*, that *he* got entangled in a failed scheme between Wolfe and Allen Dulles, and through this, Thumbert had made acquaintance with the former.

It was directly after the Office of Strategic Services had been dismantled, that I came to meet Thumbert, as previously mentioned, and I believe he had been a great help sorting things out in Nuremburg, after the War. He spent several weeks briefing William Donovan, so you could say, that he had a knack for having friends in high places: Dulles, Donovan, Reinhard Heydrich, Wernher von Braun, and in the U.S., Jack Parsons, Marlene Dietrich, Frank Sinatra, and yes, he had dinner once with Bob Hope.

I know for a fact that Thumbert was attempting to acquire funds for Jack Parsons during the spring of 1952, and had met for the last time with Parsons in late May, just weeks before Parsons was blown to pieces in his lab. Now Parsons was headed to Mexico City at the time of his untimely passing, and supposedly in route to Israel, and I know, for a fact, that Allen Dulles had grave concerns that the impoverished Parsons could *actually* be headed to Moscow.

The only photo I have of Thumbert (on right)
with Jack Parsons (left). California, May, 1952

And then, Thumbert was arrested in July (under the Mann Act), and I've always wondered, if Thumbert had been arranging Parsons' fleeing the U.S., by the favors of the USSR, as a kind of double-agent skullduggery. I do know that he hated everything about the communists, but Thumbert had mentioned to me more than once, how small the world was growing, and his shock over the assassination of Trotsky in Mexico, and he expressed his fears for his own family, a brother in particular, living in Ukraine. So, who knows?

Chapter 13

There is a scene in Kubrick's *Lolita* when *Humbert* takes leave of Charlotte, Jean, and the character playing me, at the town's dance. The subtlety of this event was missed, except not by me. Because Humbert suggests that he will leave us *to find cups* to drink from, and then he just disappears, doesn't bring us cups.

We find him upstairs, pensively gazing out at the kids dancing, and we are to assume that he is spying on Lolita, but this was not the case at all.

Thumbert was way *more complex* than that!

Thumbert was a great dancer, and I believe, taught all forms of dance while in Berlin. The movie, *Lolita*, portrays Clare Quilty, played by Peter Sellers, as the "star dancer" of the evening, but no, it was Thumbert. In the actual story, there was no *Clare Quilty* character. If you think about it, the Sellers character was not plausible, in *any* way, nor would "*any* man go to such lengths" just to get Lolita alone, and finally steal her away: From the hospital.

That's not what actually happened anyway.

Yolita was not twelve, not fourteen, but fifteen. She was seventeen when she met Jack Parsons in California and you could say that he "stole her" from Thumbert, but I know for a fact that Thumbert was not opposed, maybe initially, maybe he was talked into it, from all sides.

Thumbert was more broad-minded than given credit for.

Thumbert, in my opinion, was possessed by a special kind of genius, not appreciated, not seen, not awarded prizes by society. He phoned *me* specifically, to discuss Yolita spending the summer in

California, said *Yolita thought Parsons* was *genius*, and I had to laugh out loud. Parsons was the genius of the *new* world, and to which Yolita might gravitate, for sure.

Thumbert was *old* world developed, and think about it, what *teen* girl appreciates French literature, subtle themes, big concepts, religion? This *was* the inner brain within Thumbert, so when he disappeared at the dance in the Kubrick movie, to get cups, and we find Thumbert staring-out across the gymnasium at the young dancers, can I tell you what was being ignited, within that juxtaposition of a mind such as Thumbert's with such an event? Was Nazi Germany likewise on his mind, contrasting this gymnasium in Des Moines? Perhaps czarist Russia?

He wasn't oogling the girls that evening, that I know, all wrong in the film, *Lolita*.

Thumbert was equally mad of brain, as a young fellow like Parsons was mad of brain, and later, with Yolita thrown into the mix, all mad, and all of it, an accidental mix of genius.

Parsons with Yolita, Topanga Creek, spring 1952

Chapter 14

I spent many long hours alone with Thumbert between 1950 and 1953 (nursing my drink) and I can confess that I would not have remembered our conversations if he wasn't one to repeat himself. Returning home, I always made notes to myself, to include in my reports.

And really, he was *a professor*. He often lectured me privately, and these lectures I sometimes found somewhat interesting, particularly as long as the bourbon was flowing.

You could feel it coming on, from a stirring, deep excitement, rising to the surface of Thumbert's leaning posture, and manifested as a half-winking glint in Thumbert's eye, whereupon he might state these two Latin words: *Translatio imperii*.

He'd glance over at me, confirming that I was a willing party, like he was strapping-on my seat belt; strapping me onto a rollercoaster-ride into what was *really* on his mind.

"These two words have caused more misery to humanity than any others," he said, as if he had memorized this opening line for a classroom lecture. I would be staring intently at him, and he could feel my stare, but his eyes were not looking back at me, nor focused on anything in particular.

Suddenly, he would turn, look me in the eye, and say with a scowled expression: "Catherine de' Medici."

Then, I was to nod, as if I understood, for him to continue.

He would say, "Queen of France!"

Another nod from me, then he'd continue: "1547 to 1559. A contemporary to who?"

Ah yes, a signal of his, to allow me another sip on my drink. What was coming, was soliloquy.

He'd smile slyly and say, "Maaaartin Luther." Then, "Who ELSE?"

His answer: "King Hennnry VIII."

I'd take another sip, then he'd say: "The king! 1491 to 1547. What tumult, this period!"

I recall this fairly precisely, because I had heard this lecture more than once. He'd ask me, "Do those dates sound *familiar*?"

This was my signal to recite back to him the more-basic facts: "Yes, 1492, *Columbus sailed the ocean blue.*"

Satisfied that I was still listening, he'd ask, "Is this making sense to your formally-inadequate American understanding?"

Then I would say, "*Translatio imperii*?"

His reply, always, "Yesssss."

Thumbert had many lecture topics. Sometimes he would say, "*Translatio imperii*: Lorenzo Valla." Or Tacitus. Or Arminius. Or Abraham! Or Caesar! Vespasian! Constantine!

I may have heard all about Catherine de' Medici four times. That she was married at age fourteen to a king of the same age, fourteen, and that this was arranged by the Catholic pope, also a Medici. He found it fascinating how three centuries of Valois family rule over France ended with Catherine outliving her three sons, all three crowned King, then no more Valois.

I think it was the Bourbon court after Valois, until the Revolution, then Napoleon, then Bourbon, then another Napoleon, then a Bourbon, etc.

Each lecture I heard three times, or four, just to say, that I became quite familiar with Thumbert's lecture topics, as I'm sure Yolita became familiar with them, as well, poor girl.

Once he said: *"Translatio imperii--* Jack Parsons!" Parsons was the anti-linear secessionist who bucked all authority and paid the ultimate price. This was near the end of my work with Thumbert, not long after he had met Parsons. I only heard that lecture on Parsons once, but I never forgot it.

Chapter 15

We cannot interpret Thumbert apart from his birth to age-eighteen in czarist Russia. In many ways, I listened to him because I felt sorry for him.

Thumbert's lectures revolved around a theme, for how he had been tracing history, and interpreting it through his own strange-head. His thoughts ranged from illuminating to nonsensical. Certain things about America baffled him, particularly his students. He would say, "Literature solves *the puzzle*."

He'd say, "You can't read Victor Hugo without a deeper curiosity about France. To understand France, we must untangle the Catholics from the Protestants. This thread leads us to where?"

This was my cue to look up from my drink, say emphatically, "Rome."

"Yessss," he'd reply as if we were on this train of thought together.

"And we can't even catch a GLIMPSE of Rome, if we can't see Germany to the north, nor the sacking of Rome by these *barbarians*, nor appreciate the greatness of the Romans, only because historians, especially the Catholics, leave out the most important parts of it."

He'd lean forward again, look at me. I was being called upon to say, "Oh! And what was that?"

"The ancient Romans saw the barbarians advancing in power, centuries ahead. We always have got to have *barbarians* coming, but in this case, the threat was *real*, and why can't WE see it?"

"This is our clue," Thumbert said, "*Who wrote-out* the ancient Germans from OUR history? It was the ROMANS, so this is obvious: Who writes the history?"

"The victors! The *Roman Catholics*."

Now he was talking once again to himself, emphatically stating: "Trickery!"

"You would think that we'd want to know what the French have to say, because by now, by 1500, they have seen it *all*; every bickering family of Europe across the centuries."

"The kings and queens, can they see it? Absolutely not! The peasants? No! It's only found in the literature, in the paintings, in the culture, in the *joie de vivre*! Now we can find this same thing in Russia, in Dostoyevsky, but where is this *in America*? I wish you could stand next to me in my classroom, observe the *blank stares* looking back at me. I'd rather teach in a barnyard!"

Politely, he'd include me in his diatribe for the sake of relevance:

"Remember when you, and Jean, and Charmin, tracked me down and found me watching the American children dancing together in the gymnasium? What did I see? Dostoyevsky! *This* is what I watch! And this is what I teach! Not names! Not dates! Not literature! But how to *see*!"

Now me, I liked the booze, and I liked the women, and Thumbert smoked his pipe, as many gentlemen tended to do, but he only lit-up at home, in the study, never around the women, but I imagine he smoked his pipe around Yolita, as well. By now, at this juncture in the telling, his pipe would have gone out, and this was all part of the performance, the tapping of his pipe over a ceramic tray to remove the ashes, and while packing it again, he might repeat intently, as if he just realized I was there, still listening, "But how *to see*, you see."

Then he would strike a wooden match, light his pipe again, stare off into space, as if I wasn't there, except I was, watching, as if from through a keyhole. What a show!

"What is *the trickery* you always mention?" I asked him once.

"THIS IS the question, isn't it, John? Now you too are on the same path as me, aren't you? Poor fellow!"

Yolita with a graduate student at Cal Tech
Summer, 1952

Now Thumbert's pipe was again lit, on fire, wafts of smoke hanging in the air, as I was leaning forward, and he reclined, continuing, "The TRICKERY is not the EXCEPTION, but this is the wheels upon which history proceeds. Louis XVI was an honest man and what was he tricked by? *Translatio imperii!* Marie Antoinette also, John. An honest, poor woman."

Thumbert said, "'Let them eat cake,' is how we remember her, and this too, is *trickery*. And how do we know of this? They chopped off her head! And they had *a device* invented for this very thing! Who BUILDS such a device? Would *you*?"

He leaned forward, glanced partially in my direction, to check if I had not fallen asleep, which I sometimes would do, only to rouse again several minutes later to note that he was still talking in soliloquy, *don't mind me*!

He continued: "Marie Antoinette, being led up to the scaffold, stepped on her executioner's foot. Of course, she was nervous, who wouldn't be? Notice this, what does she say? 'Pardon me.'"

He chuckles, "Not the final words of *a tyrant*!"

"And why?! And for what?! How do these things happen?! And it's happening right now! THIS is French literature. And all literature and painting and poetry, tragedy, comedy, irony, yes, even Sartre, Camus, so much! Summed-up within these two words of a queen, 'Pardon *me*!'"

Thumbert is tapping his pipe again. He continues, "These two words, are they a finality? No, this is our clue. But a clue to what? The trickery! You see it, John? What part of 'Pardon me," is remembered? I'll tell you! THIS we must *see* or we will be destined to be exactly as Marie Antoinette. Why? Because she could not see it, any more than my students, but see *what*?"

He taps his pipe again, asks, "What is *it*? Proper *logic*, applied to falsification, John. This begat that. Straight out of the *Book of Daniel*. And these children, in America, should know the *Book of Daniel*, and this is no small thing. That they don't know the *Book of Daniel*. They don't know Marie Antoinette. And they don't know a thing about ancient Germany, either."

He continued, "A student asked me once, no doubt a Christian, 'Don't you mean, we don't know God from the *Book of Daniel* and we don't know *Jerusalem*?'"

"I replied to this student, 'You don't know Germany and you underestimate Rome. Then how can you know Jerusalem? Everything you know about Jerusalem comes through Rome.'"

"I asked this student, 'Who writes the history? Answer me that. And that's *your* answer.'"

Thumbert is again lighting freshly packed tobacco, concludes this oratory for the evening:

"It's purposefully obscured. You might think my Protestant Anglo-Saxon students could even be curious, and yet, all curiosity has been washed out of them. Who did this to them? Rome? The *Book of Daniel*? A revolution? Lenin? Stalin? The Roosevelts? The Rockefellers? Me? You? God? The Chariots of Fire?"

"Yes, John, yes, can we say yesss?"

The soliloquy then ignited for one last burst, "My sense is that my students are aware of 'but one' revolution, a very small revolution as revolutions go. Now France, Russia, Germany, THESE were revolutions."

"What revolution did the Protestants ignite? This would be wonderful to know, and we wouldn't know, could we, if the Catholics write the history for the Protestants."

"They tell me, '*Teach*!' They say, 'Teach our children *well*!'" Thumbert concluded.

"I say, 'Feed them on *your* DREAMS? No, if I told them, they will cry. And so, can we ever become *ourselves*?'"

"No, just look at them, and you will sigh.'"

Thumbert tapped his pipe again, said to me, "Ah, but I see again that I've worn you out, John. We will pick this up another night and I thank you for being a most gracious listener. I feel so much more lively when I have an audience."

Chapter 16

The authorities that exist have been established by God. Consequently, he who rebels against the authority is rebelling against what God has instituted, and those who do so will bring judgement on themselves. For rulers hold no terror for those who do right, but for those who do wrong. Romans 13:1

I recall Thumbert's lecture that began with *Translatio imperii* and then he'd say: "Romans 13."

This was the one topic which varied by its content, sometimes included a soliloquy on the works of Victor Hugo as representative of *rebellion*. Other times he took a tangent to discuss the Jews and their rebellion leading to the destruction of the Temple in Jerusalem by a certain Roman general, Vespasian, and his son, Titus. Once this led to Napoleon and his innovative use of the military cannon which decimated France's enemies and extended its empire.

I knew nothing about any of it. What can I say? Who actually studies the Bible? Nor had I heard of the French author, Victor Hugo, and I suppose was a French politician, but he'd say: "1885 — the year of Hugo's death, the greatest funeral Europe had ever seen, at the Pantheon of Paris, over two *million* mourners in attendance."

After Thumbert was arrested in 1953 on charges which made no sense, certainly not murder, and his manuscript was completed, which he had sent to Scribner's, among others, his own manuscript was returned to him, not via the mail, but thrown down, slapped on a small table, in a small interrogation room, his manuscript revised, with the new title, *Lolita*.

They told him, "Read it!"

This was prior to Nabokov being brought in, prior to *Lolita's* translation into French. *Lolita* was sloppy, vastly more pornographic, because Thumbert flipped through his revised manuscript, having already guessed what this was: Blackmail.

Still, this left him speechless. They said to him, "Well …?"

He told me, that he then looked his captors in the eye, replied, "*Translatio imperii*."

These men had not read *Lolita* themselves, they had no clearance for that, so what might have been discussed, the manuscript itself, was not.

Silence. Intimidation. *Lolita* was picked-up, stuffed back into the large manila envelope from which it came, and the men silently left the room.

Oh! I nearly forgot— written upon the envelope in large, bold lettering, not escaping Thumbert's attention: Operation Lolita.

Yolita catching 40 winks
Photo by Jack Parsons, 1952

Chapter 17

Now I have had nearly an entire decade to reflect on it, after my involvement, during which I came to appreciate that Thumbert had anticipated his removal, his failure, as most well-intended endeavors end in some form of arrest, obfuscation and obscurity, or in the vernacular, Thumbert Thumbert was relegated to the dust bin. Even while I participated in the very things which led to Thumbert's arrest, I was just doing my job, passing time, collecting a paycheck, while Thumbert was equally undermining the system, by his educating of ME.

I do not believe there remains a single copy of Thumbert's *Yolita*, while *Lolita*, perhaps ten, twenty-million copies have been rolled-off the presses, a huge success, and I alone knew this to be another fatal flaw of history.

I washed my hands of *Lolita* when the book came out in 1955.

One day, in 1957, I happened to see the cover of a travel magazine, and pictured was the Dardanelles cannon, which today is housed in Great Britain. It was as if a button was pressed within my mind and I could recall the entire lecture made by Thumbert on Victor Hugo, Napoleon III, and Romans 13.

Of course, Thumbert himself was long dead at the time, four years having passed, but here, in a flash, HIS WORDS were living on, within *me*. You might think that I appreciated him in that moment, but no, I hated him for what he had done to me. He had corrupted ME, while Yolita, he had *never* corrupted.

Yes, I was angry. I even had a nightmare, in 1957, after seeing the photo of the Dardanelles cannon, because I saw it again in my dream. Except the cannon was fractured, and people were afraid, and others in charge were there, asking who had done this, who cracked this cannon? And everyone was looking to me. And I wasn't sure, if I had an answer, in my dream or if I was — to blame.

Then I felt the cannon's weight on my chest, which woke me, and I sat up and the nightmare was so real that I marveled that I *could* sit up, with such a heavy gun placed upon my chest.

Chapter 18

Thumbert's studies were in French literature, yes, but this was his formal training.

As mentioned, he delved into all topics of interest to him. His knowledge of *the cannon* as a weapon of choice across Europe's modern centuries was still relevant when it came to the Nazis, Stalin, Churchill, Roosevelt, and the CANNON; which Thumbert referred to as *propulsion*. And *propulsion* was why he ultimately came to America, and was spying on somebody, either for Germany, Russia, England or the United States; possibly even spying *on me* while I was spying on him.

What was *it* that Thumbert wanted me to know? Not dates. Not places. Not any of the usual focusses of teaching attention, yet something else. All the content of every soliloquy he gave was for one purpose. To illustrate. And what were these illustrations about? Every lesson featured *a thread*. He was teaching me how to follow a thread.

A curiosity about this methodology is another, often missed, aspect of any story—the beginning and the ending. Thus, every thread has a beginning and an ending. I once commented on this to Thumbert, as he had paused speaking to pack his pipe with more tobacco.

I asked, "I understand that you are unwinding a thread, but how did you know *where* to begin?"

Thumbert explained, that he was sent to study the Dardanelles gun in England, which was supposedly cast in bronze in 1464 as a siege gun for the Ottoman army at Constantinople.

The Dardanelles Cannon

How and why did this enormous cannon get transported from Turkey to London?

The Royal Navy learned of this cannon in 1807, apparently after the Turks had fired projectiles from it, causing an alleged 28 casualties to the British. Sketches of the cannon from 1807 depict a huge cylindrical pipe (weighing 37,000 pounds), still lying like an ancient relic left behind on the ground, likely *too heavy* to move by the technologies of the time in 1807.

The iron projectile balls would have been as wide as a yardstick. Who knows how much gunpowder it would have required to blow-out a ball of such weight, balls that could not be *lifted* by human strength alone, then the barrel accurately aimed for the ball to travel much distance. Thumbert was sent to London in 1938 by the Nazis to study it as a part of "a big-guns project" designing the German battleship, *Bismarck*.

Thumbert reported back to the Blohm & Voss shipyard that the Dardanelles gun was not a cannon at all. He told them that siege cannons must be moved from their foundry and this was too large, cumbersome, and heavy for even forty oxen to transport. In fact, it was so heavy that it was forged *in two pieces* with a screw mechanism to link them together. Thumbert calculated it would have *blown the two sections apart* if enough force was generated to launch any projectile from it.

Blohm & Voss concurred. Thumbert had said, there would not have been a means available in 1464 to screw two-such pieces together, and Blohm & Voss said, yes, and how could the alignment of the rifling assure the projectiles did not impact the fall height. In other words, the cannon, on the battlefield, would have been *impossible* to screw its two pieces together securely, for the cannon to not have become *a bomb* itself.

Thumbert also noted, four places for *gears* to turn this great cylinder, and suspected that it was part of an ancient machine, not a cannon at all.

Now I have told you this STORY and what is *the thread*?

You didn't realize there would be a test!

It's fine if you missed it, because I fully missed it myself.

First of all, this piece of ancient machinery was *found* lying in the ruins of Constantinople. The British likely stumbled upon it in 1807, finding no explanation for it.

What's the beginning *of the thread*? "Something which has no explanation" is given an explanation. If it's *not* a cannon, then the story about the cannon being forged in 1464 is a lie, as is, its use by the Ottomans against the British in 1807.

None of this history could have been true, if we are *not* looking at a cannon.

And, not only does the average person know nothing about cannons, nor about the Ottoman empire dating back to 1464, the

81

average person BELIEVES it's a cannon, and why? Because it was given as a gift to Queen Victoria, and if Queen Victoria says that it's a cannon, by God, it's a cannon.

Where does this thread end, if we have a beginning and a middle? It ends with the realization that we are continually sold lines of a false narrative which serve another purpose.

We come to the end of this story: A certain sultan, happened to learn of the Dardanelles cannon, at Constantinople, and what does Constantinople represent, if not Eastern power? Which power? *See it? The name? Constantine?*

The thread is about observing the *deceit*, woven through the history taught to the unquestioning. The cannon provides an illustration for how tricks are made.

The "illustrated" Dardanelles gun
looks nothing like the original.

More on this thread:

1) Why did Constantine divide his empire and move the capitol of Rome to Constantinople? To thwart the barbarians from the North intending to sack *Rome*.

2) Then there is Constantinople itself and mystery-artifacts found in the ruins.

3) One of these mysteries was a gigantic iron cylinder featuring gear tracks, claimed to be a siege cannon, yet the details don't line-up with common sense.

4) One aspect which makes no sense is that "a cannon" forged in 1464 could be repurposed in 1807 (343 years later) to fire cannon balls at the British Navy.

5) The drawings of this huge cylinder from 1807 show it still lying in rubble, so *when* was it fashioned back into "a workable cannon"?

6) The sultan who gave this cannon to Queen Victoria, could have just sent her a postcard from Constantinople. Why would he go to the trouble to have this 37,000 lb. cylinder transported to London as a gift and why would she want it?

7) The cylinder offers no practical purpose. If the cannon was so amazing, why didn't Great Britain put this 37,000 lb. cannon back into service for the military?

8) The cannon is valuable to Queen Victoria only for the story around it, which a) Distracts us from unexplainable enormous machine parts discovered from antiquity and b) Supports the narrative that Great Britain is the greatest empire with the greatest weapons, ever.

9) One aspect of the British narrative was that King Henry VIII defied the grip of the Catholic church over England and this piece of scrap metal symbolizes Protestant religious defiance, as Constantinople likewise represents Roman defiance.

10) Why must this thing be shipped half-way across the planet to be put on display in the Tower of London? Because it's a powerful phallic symbol of the Victorian empire.

11) Lastly, the Dardanelles gun came to be a gift from Queen Victoria to the people of Great Britain, a gun which has nothing to do with the people of Great Britain, except it's the stories we tell ourselves which matter to us the most, so look at this gun, and marvel, not at the gun, but at the stories we tell ourselves.

"What a fine gift for me," says the queen, Victoria, what a fine *symbol*, to possess a CANNON from Constantinople. A cannon, which fired upon the bravest of brave Royal Navy in 1807, the largest cannon ever made, which cannot stop the Royal Navy.

"Anglo-Saxon victory" over Rome, in Constantinople, is what this cannon represents. If the cannon had been found in Iowa, Queen Victoria would have said, "Don't bother with it."

But REALLY, the cannon is clearly, NOT a cannon, but let's not spoil the queen's narrative. Other strange objects were likely found lying in the ruins of Constantinople, dating back to antiquity, but much-lighter relics, relics of machines, and these were carried off, never to be seen again.

Thumbert told me: "History is like a roulette wheel, always tilted in favor *of the house.*"

And Thumbert told me that the Nazis laughed out loud when they found out that the Dardanelles gun was not a cannon. And they said, "We will show the Brits what a cannon is."

Chapter 19

Yolita at Malibu Beach, 1952

Thumbert was a master sleuth and it took me a while to catch on, with whom I was dealing.

He never wasted a minute.

He possessed many, many books, which he eventually had shipped from Berlin, many covering the history of Europe. Thumbert could walk into a room, scan the details, within two minutes tell you everything about the occupant, including their detailed ancestry, and be spot on.

Other times he could speak of things just plain nutty.

He said he could boil down the contents of the *Encyclopedia Britannica* into "a summary of everything" within a single-page folded-pamphlet. And the rest of the encyclopedia was rubbish. Thumbert told me that he spent an hour with Goebbels, and gleaned this ability of reduction, and simplification, from him.

Thumbert said, "There's not many tricks in the book of tricks, because the tricksters take the ones proven to work, and simply apply them to any topic, over and over again."

For example, the repetition of falsified facts, embedded within other proven facts, is a trick of the pharmaceutical giants. "If they had their way," he said, "They'd have the people swallowing an aspirin each and every day." Then, they'd *also* be treating the side-effects of the aspirin.

Thumbert said, "Under such a model, an industry could capture an entire nation's GDP within a few short decades, and I believe they will."

When Thumbert first heard the term, "The Third Reich," Thumbert said, "I had to smile. You can't be the ones to *start* The *First* Reich, that just won't fly with the people. So, it's the *Third* Reich."

"This embeds the false reality into an accepted history."

He told me that Americans, despite what they believe, participate more within a Fourth American Reich than a First Reich. The *roots* to the *idea* of American freedom go way deeper than George Washington or the *Mayflower*.

Chapter 20

Today's date is August 12, 1962. Of my many friends across the globe, I can assume that at least *one* has been watching me and reporting my activities to headquarters. I am certain now that Thumbert must have known, that part of my job, was to spy on him, but at the time I thought that Jean and I had the perfect cover.

We might look back, believe that 1962 is within a kind of Golden Age. That is, if we ignore *our threads*.

Thumbert and I never discussed this undercover part of our lives. So, when he told me in 1953, that first week he was in prison, that he had written a manuscript, I just nodded my head, yes, it made sense. Would I make this revealed fact known to the Terminal Island warden? He knew that they already knew about it, but I was not informed about this, because you know it's a test, to see if I'll come forward with this information.

If I do come forward to my superiors that Thumbert is WRITING, they'll know I'm doing by job. If I don't come forward, then my behavior, my protection of Thumbert, could be somewhat suspicious.

Like Beria's quote, Stalin's secret police chief, "Show me the man and I'll show you the crime."

You might say, don't make them suspicious of you. But in our game, it's better if those around you ARE suspicious of you, gives you more leeway if you aren't following orders to a tee.

I was loyal to Thumbert as a PERSON, but he had been screwing-up lately; now he's a liability to me. But if I start covering my ass, they'll really get suspicious. So you play it cool. I'm not going to report that Thumbert is submitting from his jail cell, a tell-all manuscript to New York publishers regarding American intelligence operations since World War II.

He said, "It's a kind of travel diary about Yolita and me."

I laughed.

I asked, "What could you write about Yolita in your book?"

Then he said, "I'm charged with 'industrial espionage'. To make it stick, I'm also charged under the Mann Act. All tied to the Jack Parsons thing. They imagine that I was trying to help Jack get to the USSR via Israel."

"Were you?"

"They're slapping me on the wrists. They know there's not a shred of truth to it. My lawyer will get me out of here, probably next week if things go well."

"Jesus, Thumbert. Is *this* what you've been writing about?"

Thumbert replied, "I write to amuse myself. I've gone through three reams of paper, but I'm not anybody. Nobody cares if I keep requesting more paper."

I said, "If they suspect that you have sympathies for the communists, then to them, you are not a nobody."

He asked if I could do him a special favor. Could I take one of his hand-written manuscripts, have it typed, and would I mail it to a certain literary agent? He said that he couldn't mail anything from the prison without it first crossing prying-eyes and the warden's desk.

This favor was putting everything on the line. If I helped him smuggle out his manuscript, it was too obvious that it was *me*. I told him, "There's just no way ..."

He said, waving me to shut-up, "I already knew your answer. But I had to ask. You're not my ONLY friend, John. But you are my friend, aren't you?"

I replied, "I know that you are my friend -- and a mentor. Whatever you need, I'm there for you. Tobacco? What do you need? A listening ear? But I'm not going to do anything that makes *me* your fellow cellmate."

After I returned to my hotel, I got on the phone, dialed my supervisor, to update him, of course, which was my job.

Chapter 21

The beatniks are taking us over in 1962, not the Soviets.

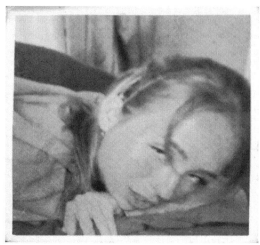

Yolita, Haight-Ashbury, Christmas, 1951

I spoke to Yolita last year. She called me! Apparently, I'm listed in the phone book. I asked her, how she was, where she was. She said, "San FRAN Cisco, bay-bee!"

I wanted to ask her what she thought of *Lolita*, the Kubrick film version, but I didn't. I know she read half-of Nabokov's tale, said she had to put it down, called it trash. It was not even *her*, not her mind, no depth, animalistic, nothing in it, nothing about Jack Parsons. She likely wouldn't even tell her friends that she is Lolita, but no, she is Yo.

To tell her friends would only highlight, I'd think, that she is no longer a *nymphet*, downhill to thirty.

A little backstory about me: During the War, I had just completed basic training; Marines. I was taken aside, removed from my unit, transferred to the relatively new OSS.

Office of Strategic Services.

I was made an aide (to an aide) serving the great U.S. colonel, William J. Donovan, famous, you know him, so I won't elaborate. Donovan is the only soldier (since World War I) to have been awarded all FOUR military decorations: The Medal of Honor, The Distinguished Service Cross, The Distinguished Service Medal, and The Distinguished Security Medal, plus a Silver Star and Purple Heart, and more.

I am assuming you remember the film from 1940, *The Fighting 69th*, which I saw three times, based on real-life people including "Wild Bill" Donovan. So, when I was suddenly thrown into the OSS in 1944, I could not believe my luck.

Donovan in 1940 was a household name and this man hadn't even gotten STARTED saving the world from both the Nazis AND the Communists. Donovan single-handedly was all across Europe thwarting Hitler's plans to attack Russia through Ukraine, Yugoslavia and Greece; Donovan delayed the launch of *Operation Barbarossa* from May to June, 1941, which put the Krauts at Moscow just in time for an early Soviet winter.

When I say "Krauts at Moscow," I mean, 150 divisions, almost three million Nazi soldiers, 3,000 tanks, 2,500 planes, 7,000 artillery units, knocking on Stalin's door. By December, when Hitler was declaring war on the U.S., he was mad as hell over Donovan's forced delay of five weeks, because now Hitler has three million men freezing to death, while for the Russians, winter is what they know.

Hitler documented this, in his War Declaration Speech of 1941, saying: "Roosevelt some months before sent Colonel Donovan, a completely unworthy creature, to the Balkans, to Sofia and Belgrade, to engineer a rising against Germany and Italy ..."

Which caused the freezing of three million German men and their machines.

Donovan knew not the emotion of fear. In battle after battle during WWI, wounded more than once, asking, "Is that all you *got*?" He was the real-life model for John Wayne. I mean, Donovan LANDED at Normandy on D-Day, at age 60! Lay with his belly on the beach under machine-gun fire. Would Harry Truman have done that? Eisenhower, Churchill, Dulles?

In Donovan, Hitler met his match, and it's Truman's fault that America never got to experience what life could have been like under a U.S. President Donovan.

But I think, Donovan was destroyed by nefarious characters, as was Thumbert, in the exact same way that Kennedy is being destroyed, as I type these very words, and I am gravely concerned, for Kennedy, for you, and for me. Oh yes, we'll be at war again if they have their way.

Then the kids will be asking, "What are we fighting for?"

And, "Don't ask me, I don't give a damn!"

Yolita, Des Moines, 1949
In 1950, Truman sent military advisors to Vietnam.

Chapter 22

I realize that nobody will believe me. But I was there, too, at Normandy, D-Day. This started in DC. The aides were assembled, volunteers amongst the aides were requested to fly *to England* to assist in operations, and of course, I volunteered: History in the making!

Once there, I assumed that Donovan would be assisting Eisenhower on the British side of the Channel. But no, Donovan and Colonel Bruce were taking a transport, plus one aide, and again, they asked for volunteers to join the transport. Nobody stepped forward. We drew straws and I lost.

Then right there on the beachhead, I was there, lying flat on our bellies, as Donovan and Bruce were arguing over *shooting each other* in the event they were captured by the Nazis. They then looked to me, and this time I volunteered. I said, "If we're about to be captured, I'll shoot you both, then I'll shoot myself."

This was a serious negotiation.

You have to appreciate, we are lying flat, and Donovan looks at Bruce, Bruce at Donovan, then Donovan says to me, big grin, "No, I'll shoot *you*, and I'll shoot Bruce, then *I'll* shoot myself."

This represents the kind of trust he placed in himself. I mean, if Eisenhower, or Truman, or LBJ, were lying there with us, Donovan would have made the same arrangements; he goes last. The only way he could trust that the job gets done right.

And this was why a rift developed between Donovan and Dulles, the subtle dynamics, such as *who will shoot who* first and who can be trusted. And so, I trusted Donovan, had zero trust in Allen Dulles.

You ask me, how is it that President Kennedy came to name the Washington airport, with the *Dulles* name? After *Republicans*? How do you say? – *"Politics* were involved."

Nobody can just waltz into the presidency of any Superpower, as Kennedy did, as a very young man, and not throw a bone to the former administration. I knew through backchannel that Eisenhower insisted on naming the airport *Dulles* and that this was a bone Kennedy was willing to throw.

The Dulles brothers were instrumental in funding Ike's campaign in the 1952 election, but that all changed after the surprise defeat of Nixon in 1960.

This name of the airport, Dulles, won't last long, I can assure you. Think about it! John Foster is long dead and Allen was ousted recently under bad terms. If the world as we know it, continues unimpeded, the Dulles name can't last; Americans will see what's happening within their own government and change course. Or surely the Yolita's of this world will be in full scale revolt.

Yolita with friend, 1948.
Charmin wrote on back, "Homely child."

Chapter 23

You might ask me, how, in God's name, is any of this relevant?

Do you want the backstory on how *Lolita* was published (yes, it's THIS complicated), and made into a movie, or don't you? Because, think about it! The Intelligence Services were investing heavily, and still does, to present a culture of *family values* to the world. This is part of the efforts to undermine *the Soviets*. That capitalism is doing just fine, one car, two cars in the garage, a chicken in the pot, a lawn to mow, hedge trimmers, etc.

Why ALLOW a book like *Lolita*, a self-critical tale ABOUT America, to see the light of day?

First of all, a book like *Lolita*, you'd want it written by *a Russian:* Nabokov.

Because *Lolita* is fiction, and Humbert, a European, with one blow, we see what happens when we allow the Russian MIND to influence the European continent, and then bring THAT to America, which is, at best *pedophilia*.

And what is the America we see in both the book, and the movie? *Victims*, if we do not beware the diabolical "Russian machinations" from without. *Lolita* is about commie subversion of 1950s America as symbolized by pedophilia.

The manipulation could be so subtle, that *Russia* could be linked to pedophilia (I mean, with a name like Vladimir and Nabokov), and we would not notice it, until Russia is in the news, blaring in our own living rooms.

In the movie, the character played by Peter Sellers, Clare Quilty, pretends to be Lolita's school psychologist. He says something very interesting to Humbert Humbert, which escaped me the first viewing. I'm not sure who put the line in the script, whether the book author, Nabokov, or the filmmaker, Kubrick, or was an improvisation by Sellers, but somebody *did* it.

Sellers is parodying a Freudian psychologist of German, Swiss or Austrian origin, and in this case, clearly is a former Nazi. Except, Sellers, we know, in the character of Quilty, is also the director of Lolita's school play.

Peter Sellers as Dr. Zempf (left)
negotiating with Humbert Humbert

What we are watching in the scene are two pedophiles negotiate about who gets to spend more time with *the little girl*.

Peter Sellers is presenting a series of lies. Humbert responds to Sellers with a parlay of *other* lies. Sellers has the advantage, because he knows about Humbert. Thus, we see Humbert manipulated. The audience is laughing, because the context of this meeting is serious in nature, which is, how a caring parent will make decisions for their child.

When the "school psychologist" is both a former Nazi *and* a pedophile.

Why are we laughing? We are thinking, "Haha, I see in that, how I coverup my own lies."

This puts down our guard, while a totally different message was sent. This German psychologist is a *recent* American immigrant. How was A NAZI hired by the U.S. educational system of the early 1950s?

Or HOW did Nazi, Wernher von Braun, become America's premier leader of rocket science and technology, and along with hundreds, and thousands, of former Nazi experts, like von Braun, and exactly like Dr. Zempf, so easily export themselves to America?

Dr. Zempf says offhandedly to Humbert: "Dr. Humbert, *WE* Americans ..."

So, what is this scene between Dr. Zempf and Humbert really saying?

"Dr. Humbert, we Americans don't care about *lies,* as long as we are keeping communists from teaching the children *their* lies."

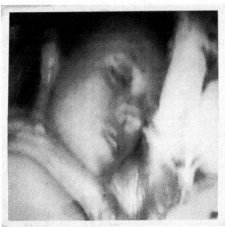

Sleeping Yolita, date unknown

Chapter 24

I, John Nearly, have not stated a single thing which you didn't already know.

But I did tell a lie. I mentioned that I had told Thumbert, that it was impossible for me to take his manuscript, have it typed, send it to his agent. And that this is what I reported to my supervisor, that no, I could not help Thumbert.

Are you kidding me? I *thanked* Thumbert for the opportunity! And why? Because it was the confession of a pedophile? No, there was not a single *jot* nor *tit* nor *tittle* in any of it. Not a nipple! It was exactly as I thought it would be, about the misappropriation of societal truth.

Chapter 25

You might be curious, as surely as I was, *what* was written in Thumbert's holy manuscript.

I wanted to know, because Thumbert had been spending so much time in California, with Jack Parsons. Was he merely spying on Parsons? Was Parsons a genius of jet propulsion, two stage rocketry, and solid fuel? Or was Thumbert interested in something else?

Would Thumbert's tell-all manuscript tell all?

Anyway, Thumbert wrote that he didn't need a WIFE; he needed CITIZENSHIP.

In other words, the Hayes-Thumbert marriage was an *arranged* marriage. As for a reward, Charmin was gifted with something she had always dreamed-of – Paris. All-expenses-paid out of an Intelligence budget to which there is no end.

Charmin was given the option to bring Yolita with her to Paris. Instead, she made arrangements for Yolita to attend boarding school in the fall, leaving Thumbert free to follow his career. He stopped teaching at Drake mid-semester because the Parsons situation required immediate intervention.

Yolita felt absolute revulsion at the idea of going away to boarding school, to which, after Charmin flew to France, it was left to Thumbert to drive Yolita to her new school. Then to wash his hands of this brief chapter of his life.

However, it was on this very road trip, that Yolita convinced Thumbert that she could learn WAY MORE from HIM, than any old boarding school. She could help him! She could learn from him, stuff! Like how to cook! And that she "could listen to his lectures." They would be trapped together in the car, seeing the country, and *learning*.

And then, down the road, Yolita would also meet Jack Parsons, and by now, Thumbert was more than willing to leave this gum-chewing, bubble-blowing, demanding *imp* behind in the care of Marjorie Cameron, Parson's girlfriend.

I think that what happened to Thumbert was that he, and Yolita, had stumbled onto a California happening already in progress, 1952 to 1953.

This photo had written on the back of it
"Marjorie—discard pile."
They must have tried to do a photo shoot,
but Yolita appears absolutely worn-out.
California, 1952

Chapter 26

Enter one, J. Edgar Hoover.

Director of the F BI.

Hoover has been in U.S. Intelligence since 1924. John F. Kennedy becomes president in 1960 with Lyndon Baines Johnson as his VP. Hoover likes his job. If Richard Nixon had won the election, Hoover's job would have remained secure, while Kennedy is letting an entrenched Hoover know that it's time to retire.

What does Texas and LBJ have to do with Massachusetts? Nothing. These are like two different countries and one might IMAGINE that this pairing was to garner more votes for the Democrats.

If I had no insider connections, I could not know that JFK was *blackmailed* into the choice of his VP. By J. Edgar Hoover and the classic manila envelope containing compromising photos of Jack.

And Robert Kennedy was furious, as was the father, Joe Kennedy, but what to do?

Now Johnson was the kind of Texan, who does what needs to be done. There's not a single Texan who doesn't know the classic LBJ style. For him to still be standing, LBJ would need to be above the law.

I'm in a position to know that Bobby Kennedy, as Attorney General, is doing everything he can to unravel LBJ's tangled web. Bobby is just a kid and possibly way over his head. Bobby aligns to Jack, while Johnson aligns to the way-more influential J. Edgar Hoover.

In other words, if something isn't done to stop the Kennedy brother's forward motion, Johnson is going down, and Hoover is going down.

Chapter 27

Thumbert's puzzlement, he infected me!

How dangerous are *ideas*!

His constant lecture theme beneath everything: *Translatio imperii.*

I could not SEE it. Then at once, the scales fall from the eyes.

Thumbert to Humbert, Yolita to Lolita, Nabokov to the Red Scare, to McCarthy, to Mao, to Dulles, to Hitler, to the unification of Germany in 1871, to Bourbon kings, to the French Revolution, to Napoleon I, to Victor Hugo, to Napoleon III, back to Catherine II, to the Protestant Reformation to Catholic control of Europe, to Martin Luther to Lorenzo Valla to Tacitus to Nero to Arminius to Jesus to Cleopatra to Caesar to a huge leap back to John F. Kennedy.

Translatio imperii.

George Washington to McKinley to Theodore Roosevelt to Roosevelt to Truman to Dulles to Eisenhower to Richard Nixon, whoops, to Kennedy. To Dulles Airport.

Through all the mistresses in-between, and all the sorrows born, since Cleopatra met Julius Caesar, to the sorrows of their son, Caesarion, to the martyrdom of Eleanor Roosevelt, to the martyrdom of Mamie Eisenhower, to Jackie and Lady Bird.

From the publishing of *Germania* to the Holy Roman Empire to the First Reich to the Second Reich to the Third Reich. To bunkers to Stalin to bunkers to Castro to bunkers.

From the Big Bang to gelatinous soup. To monkeys to Copernicus to Darwin to evolution to humanity to bunkers.

From the secret ancient wisdom tradition to Jesus to the devil to Alister Crowley to Jack Parsons to rockets to magic.

From William Burroughs to Jack Kerouac to *Dean Moriarty* to Allen Ginsberg to *Howl* and whatever else comes next, that fits fully into a tradition: To Yolita and to the beatnik-libido of her generation.

Something is happening, something *new* that this world has never seen, and what we cannot even imagine going forward from 1962.

Thumbert thought that Jack Parsons was part of what's coming next, and in my opinion, it's Ed Sullivan who is pushing the proverbial envelope.

Thumbert was determined to investigate truth in culture. Why? To put a stop to what Thumbert called the "freaking shit show of time immemorial."

However, I believe in jail, he was changing his position, using words such as "beauty" and "beautiful" and "cosmic."

Chapter 28

It would be lovely to appreciate A MIND such as Thumbert's, so we would have to appreciate that he was once born as A BABY within Imperial Russia at the beginning of the Twentieth Century. Who in America could grasp that a YOUNG MAN could SURVIVE this period of upheaval which Americans have not seen? To be there during period of the Bolsheviks, Vladimir Lenin, and the end of Imperial Romanov czarist rule.

Thumbert had a photographic memory, and the ability to PINPOINT one thing, as a center from which many spokes fanned outward. To the average Russian teenager, the photograph of the Romanov's shortly before the entire family was assassinated was simply "what was," and then suddenly what "was not."

Thumbert wanted to know how the word "Roman" had gotten into "Romanov."

Thumbert wanted to understand how "The Holy Roman Empire" got mixed into the marriages of the tsars. These were the spokes radiating from a center. He became an amateur authority on Princess Sophie of Anhalt-Zerbst of Prussia, who came to be known as Catherine the Great of Russia. Thumbert likewise wanted to know how *Russia* was mostly within the word, Prussia.

He wanted to know why Catherine was raised as a Lutheran, but converted to Russian Orthodox, and then nationalized Russian religion as the queen. During her long reign (1762-1796), she extended the borders of the Russian Empire by 200,000 square miles, including Crimea and Right-bank Ukraine. This period became known as the age of Russian Enlightenment when Russia became more of a cultural hub for Europe, than Europe itself, through the exchange of IDEAS.

King George III called upon Queen Catherine for help to suppress the rebellion in America. Hessian mercenaries were instead enlisted, who defected all across New England, but what if Catherine had sent Russian enlistees in great numbers, and *they* had defected to the colonies, as the Hessians had?

Thumbert laughed that Catherine of Russia was more of a king, than a queen, that she took on many Russian lovers, that her own son, Paul, was illegitimate. In between her duties as empress, she read on a wide range of topics, including Voltaire, with whom she kept correspondence, and she read Tacitus, described by her as the first intellectual who understood "power politics" as they are, not as they *should be*, that royalty, nor the public, act according to professed ideals, including the clergy, but all have hidden motives of self-interest.

Thus, Thumbert investigated Tacitus, also, because the life of Tacitus overlaps the First Century Christian Church (56-120 AD), the end of the Julio-Claudian Empire, with the beginning of the Flavians and the Five Good Emperors.

Thumbert's lectures were all about finding and revealing *the historical hubs*.

"The job of court historians," Thumbert would say, "Is to *adjust* the historical hubs."

Or as Edward Hallett Carr once wrote, "Study *the historian* before you begin to study the facts."

I asked him, "Please explain."

He replied, "You've not heard of the shell game?"

"Yes, but I am still confused."

He replied, "The American game of football, if this will help you to understand, the man passing the football, he is looking *one way*, while his arm passes in a different direction."

"I see," I replied, "Such as Hitler, or Goebbels, providing one impression to cover their true motives?"

"Yes, but in a different way," Thumbert explained, "Because I am referring to the telling of history, and what's the shell game? The assumption that history, is what happened in the past, so we look there, but the ball is not there. When we look within the PRESENT, the explanation of what happens today can always be found under the shell of what is not taught about the past."

"Just imagine," he said, "*History* taught to children in Nazi Germany will be nothing like the history taught to Russian children or American children or what's taught in France."

"History is not a laundry list," was another of Thumbert's favorite sayings.

History, according to Thumbert, is like a wheel with spokes or like a pebble tossed into a pond, forming ripples. He said that to understand Russia, Catherine the Great, is the hub with spokes, not the Bolsheviks, and this is what throws everybody off, why Russia can't be understood, because the Bolsheviks are not the hub, although this is what's taught to the Russian school children.

After Catherine institutionalized the Russian church, this paved the way for the Bolsheviks.

Thumbert said, "Just look at St. Petersburg. They called it Leningrad. Then Stalingrad. Soon, the Russian people will learn that historians deceived us; it was a shell game, and we'll have St. Petersburg back. Meanwhile, Catherine, who was not Russian, gives birth to a son, Paul, who is not related to Peter the Great, yet the Russian peasants will have no other ruler, than Paul."

Thumbert likewise pointed-out that the court historians tried to place Marie Antoinette as the hub from which French history unwound, which would give rise to a Napoleon, but no, Victor Hugo was the hub of France. "Observe the funeral of Victor Hugo!" Thumbert said, "Sometimes the people get it right."

Thumbert observed this same shell game with Rome, that court historians identified with Julius Caesar, as the glory. But no, he explained, the hub was Tacitus, and *the end* of the Caesars.

He said, "The glory of Rome *begins* with the death of Nero."

Thumbert continued, "Emanating from Tacitus, as truth, we see, not Caesar, not Nero, but *Vespasian*. History through the eyes of Tacitus, we see, not Constantine, not the popes, but *Vespasian*. We see, not Rome, but *Germany*. Thus, to understand Germany, we must read Tacitus; to understand Hitler, we must read Tacitus. To understand Catherine the Great, we must read Tacitus, and why? Because Catherine read Tacitus. *She* knew Tacitus was the hub."

Tacitus was her justification for stripping down the Orthodox church.

Thumbert, ending his lecture, said, "To understand *America*, it's all in Tacitus. But historians will keep moving the shells, like history is a game, which it is! And how is this obvious? Americans do not read Tacitus. When they think of Rome, they think of Caesar. Then came 'The Fall of Rome.' Who did it fall to?"

"Historians would have us to believe that Rome fell to just-nobody," Thumbert said.

*I found this photo on Thumbert's kitchen floor
with ketchup on it! Likely from another photoshoot
with Cameron in California, 1952.*

Chapter 29

Now, appreciate, that Thumbert formed a concentric circle within ME, and so I see differently the events between Thumbert's lectures from the early 1950s, to today, 1962.

I don't see Jack Kennedy as a hub from which spokes emanate, so he can easily be stripped-out and replaced.

No, Kennedy is operating *outside* the hub. Is the *actual* hub Eisenhower? Or is it General Curtis LeMay? Or is it Lyndon Johnson? Or General Donovan or Edgar J. Hoover or is it Allen Dulles or this new man, Billy Graham, or is it Henry Luce, Billy Graham's promoter of what's the flavor of the month?

Henry Luce, the mogul of such media institutions as TIME, LIFE, Fortune and Sports Illustrated? Is Henry Luce a hub? Or part of the broader shell game?

Our cultural brokers, looking one way, while passing in another.

Billy Graham, twisting terms into a form of narrative, describing ancient Roman history as *Caesar's Rome* for public consumption.

From the very pulpit telling us, "Can't you see it? *Salvation* is happening today because of what happened *then*." The crowd streaming down from their seats in a confession *that they believe* (in the evil Roman empire).

Oh yes, it's happening! From God to the Puritans. From God to the Huguenots. From God, straight to Jesus. From God to Jerusalem. From God to Abraham in some God-forbidden desert. Then, from this God-forbidden desert, all of history emanates as a carefully crafted shell game, repeated over and over until it's a solid faith-held belief.

From God to The Beginning. From God straight to Billy Graham. *Translatio imperii* framed in a new light, to be shared unto the uttermost parts. It's brilliant, if we thought about it.

"For God so loved the world," yes, it's truth! Why it was wrapped within historical illusion spoils it; the people go home, don't understand their own leaky conversion within the broader shell game. Saved? From whom? Saved? From *ourselves*?

What was it they missed? No time to think! Bomb Mao Zedong! Bomb Pyongyang!

The historians will tell us that Billy Graham sat above the American-system-of-politics as an evangelical presidential advisor. Really?!

Bomb Hanoi!

Bomb Havana!

That's "from God" straight to the ears of Allen Dulles, to Henry Luce, to Billy Graham to an unsuspecting public which has lined-up its unflinching support.

Is there anybody ALIVE who can stand opposed to this great wind? Ah yes, *Kennedy*. He's standing up to it. And that's what I mean: This unfortunate man's time is short for this world, while Billy Graham will live on forever.

Chapter 30

The presidency of the United States, Thumbert called a false hub.

The bombing of Pearl Harbor by the Japanese, he called a false hub.

Mao Zedong, he called a true hub; Stalin a false hub.

Where was Thumbert getting his intel?

Thumbert continually advocated that what could be dug out from obscurity, that was an indicator of a hub; anything too obvious was the shell game. In other words, most of what's praised by historians, is the shit show.

Lucifer, the devil, God, Adam and Eve feeling shame in the Garden, the shit show.

The shit show is made super easy to swallow unless one actually looks into it.

I asked Thumbert once, if you discount everything of importance to humanity, what remains? I mean, why should we care about "hubs" and "spokes," if we'll *never* get it right? This would make the very logical structures and foundations of the human mind nothing but a swindle.

He laughed, in a way I have never seen him laugh, replied while tapping his pipe, "If you believe that man came from a monkey, you've been swindled. If you believe in the Garden of Eden, you've been swindled. To be or not to be, is that really THE QUESTION?"

Now his pipe was barely lit, but he puffed on it several times, leaned forward, looking directly at me, said, "I could answer that one for you, Johnny, and I'd tell you, but you would not believe me, so …

there you have it. Don't take it personally, John, to get it, you'd need to have just one original idea within your own head."

I certainly was doing all I could to muster an original thought!

Thumbert tapped his pipe, added, "What do they say? All philosophy is just footnotes to Plato?"

"What if you were the philosopher Descartes, you give a lecture, say "I think, therefore I am." He receives a standing ovation. He says to the adoring audience, 'Thank you, but anything I have spoken is merely a footnote to Plato.'"

"Now *Plato* is giving a lecture next door, so the crowd attending Descartes' lecture, all run next door. Plato receives a standing ovation, says to the adoring audience, 'Thank you, but anything I have said is merely a footnote to Socrates."

"I met a man who had been in three different European wars," Thumbert continued. "During each one he had been captured, sat-out the rest of the war in prison camps. I said to him, 'That's one way to tour Europe, isn't it?' The man replied, "Aye, I'm in *the footnotes* of history, aren't I?'"

As Thumbert and I were shaking hands good-night, he suddenly gripped my hand, jerked me forward so his mouth was at my ear. In a tone of seriousness, he said, "I've been pulling your leg, Johnny. Fuck the footnotes. There's too many. These are *my* dragons to slay."

He pushed me away with a slap on my back, said: "They're not your dragons!"

Chapter 31

The next time I sat with him, I said, "Thumbert, I know these are not my dragons to slay, but I *am* curious about this thing you call *translatio imperii*. Is it *a cause* or a footnote?"

The illustration he gave to me was how the Spanish conquistadors utilized *translatio imperii* as a primal *cause*.

Thumbert's story was about an Inca ruler in Peru named Sayri Tupac during the mid-1500s.

The Spanish invaded Peru and the ruling emperor there, Manco, met with the Spanish to bridge some form of peace. What the Spanish did, was to crown Manco with the title of emperor, which proved to be meaningless, after the Spanish continued their mistreatment of the Inca, resulting in Manco attacking the Spanish with a large army of Inca warriors.

Manco was eventually killed, so Sayri, his young son, became the ruler (with regents) of the Neo-Inca State in remote Vilcabamba. After ten years, the Spanish Viceroy offered Sayri ownership of *land* and *houses* in Cuzco if he surrendered, but Sayri did not agree to the offer. The conquistadors wanted more control over the indigenous natives, so they continued to coax Sayri from hiding.

On January 5, 1558, Sayri Tupac arrived in Lima, riding in a litter with 300 attendants and was received by Spanish Viceroy Hurtado. The condition of this peace was that Sayri had to renounce his claim to the Inca Empire, and accept baptism as a Catholic, after which, he was to be given a new Spanish name, *Diego*.

Sayri was weary of war, said okay, received a full pardon and new estates, plus a special dispensation from Pope Julius III, which allowed the repentant Diego to marry his own sister. Two years later,

Diego died suddenly and mysteriously, and his brother took control of Vilcabamba, also baptized into the Catholic church.

Thumbert asked, "Where are *the Inca* today?"

There is an answer for that question and it is this: The *Spanish* are the Inca.

Not that the Inca became Spanish, but the other way around. The Spanish Monarchy *became* the Inca Monarchy through *translatio imperii.*

How does that work? Sayri's renunciation gave official recognition that the Kings of Peru were replaced by the Monarchs of Spain. From then on, the Kings of Spain would be the legitimate *successors* of the Sapa Incas, commemorated, no less, by statues of Aztec and Inca Emperors at the main entrance of the Royal Palace *of Madrid.*

In turn, Inca Nobility received recognition of their titles under Spanish law, including privileges from the Crown, as long as they shall live. Somebody in Spain created laws to form the basis for Spain to steal the ownership of a Peruvian parcel of land or a village or a city or the entire nation.

Did the conquistadores see themselves as thieves? No, because they believed that Peru *belonged* under Spain, because Spain was under Rome, and Rome connected the entire planet back to God, Adam and Eve, the Garden, etc.

But what if ROME had just *made it all up*? Rome could do that! Were the seeds of a Roman religion within Julius Caesar or was this religion started sometime later? Originating sometime between the first Flavian emperor and the last? The last Flavian, being Constantine.

Once all lands are placed "under God," the representatives to that religion gain *legal* title. Caesar did not invent this method of conquest, rather was forced to gain foreign estates via the sword. Enacting the principle of *translatio imperii* proved to require much less effort.

Flavius Constantine did not invent this method of conquest either, but inherited the idea, which possibly originated with Flavius Vespasian 250 years earlier, who had brain-stormed the idea with Flavius Josephus, yet we will never know these origins, for certain.

This is strategic and contained in the words of Jesus, who says, "Render up to Caesar, what is Caesar's. Render up to God, what is God's." After Constantine, the Roman empire will advance under the cloak of tricking their worst enemies into "rendering unto God."

The Protestants stole this same trick.

This is why the Bolsheviks were considered so dangerous, because they were returning what was God's to the people. Under *translatio imperii*, the Romanov's ruled Russia, until a few revolutionary intellectuals saw through the game. Except it was Catherine the Great who had first seen through the game, then laughed the whole thing off, bearing an illegitimate heir and cancelling the *Roman* Eastern Orthodox church.

The Americans had taken over Cuba previous to Castro through *translatio imperii* and Castro is telling the Americans to shove it. Thus, this battle is between the hubs of a politic nearly impossible to see: Jack Kennedy versus the C IA, while the C IA is intimidating indigenous peoples, who are claiming back their rights to autonomy and ownership, especially in Cuba, backed by Communist Party ideals/missiles.

Joseph Kennedy had advocated for appeasement of Hitler, and all of Jack's Joint Chiefs of Staff, no doubt, never forgot how the elder

Kennedy was quoted in the *Boston Globe* in 1940, saying, "Democracy is finished in England. It may be here."

Is Jack *fleshing-out* his father's appeasement policy now two decades later?

Who is bucking what?

Chapter 32

The Americans believe that they OVERTHREW *translatio imperii* in their revolution and are blind to notice that America formed as an extension of Europe, with its same religions. Were English colonizers so different from Spanish conquistadors? We might ask of the Inca, the same question which we could ask of the Lakota: "Where did you go? What happened to your people and their customs?"

Thumbert pointed out that there is nobody to BLAME, and to not get off on that tangent, because a full pardon was granted, to the Inca. A full pardon was granted, to Spain, by the pope. And a full pardon is being granted right now by Billy Graham, to America.

My guess is that we shall see more of this preacher spreading forgiveness across the land, from the president, to the Congress and the Halls of Freedom, to the smallest child. Thumbert said, "It's all fine and good, if that's the best we can do."

Chapter 33

My First Lecture

I'm calling this chapter my first lecture, by John Nearly.

Thumbert is dead.

I tried to get more information about what had happened, both at the prison, and through the ranks, but nobody could tell me. One reply was that he hanged himself in his cell. The other was that he was shot while attempting to escape.

The first time I visited him in prison, he was being escorted down the hall in handcuffs by two guards, and he hollered at me, "I'm just a patsy!" Then he winked and I knew exactly what he meant.

The trial of Socrates. Tried for "corruption of the youth," for speaking against the status quo.

Now Tacitus was born in 56 AD. He is remembered as the greatest Roman historian, and this would be odd, because from our vantage, history hadn't even happened yet.

For historical perspective, NERO was emperor at the time of his birth.

This was a pivotal period for Rome, because Nero was *the last* in the line of Caesar.

We can recall that Jesus knew of Caesar, because Jesus mentions him directly: "Render unto Caesar the things that are Caesar's, and to God the things that are God's."

Christians can interpret this in a variety of ways, except one, and I'll explain.

Caesar was *not* ruling Rome during the time of Jesus. (Tiberius was emperor.)

So when Jesus uses the name of *Caesar*, Jesus is speaking *in code*. Also, at the time of Jesus, the backdrop to the story is that God came to Earth and was born in a humble manger. This was in Israel, and at the time, Israel was in widespread rebellion against Rome.

This wasn't like the American rebellion, because Israel was crushed; as was their concept of a coming messiah. What was saved out of all that, was THE CONCEPT of a coming messiah, which was brought back to Rome. In what form was "the messiah concept" brought back to Rome? It was brought back to Rome in the form of a person, a Jewish scholar-survivor, renamed Flavius Josephus.

Josephus moved *into* the emperor's palace in Rome.

Remember this trick, and it's a trick, in the same way that Washington International Airport is named Dulles; the name says what the nation's capitol is really about. To the Romans, the name Flavius speaks volumes. Because the famous later emperor, Constantine, is likewise *Flavius* Constantine. "Flavius" is like the name of "being on the same team."

What does Flavius Constantine introduce to the then-known world? The *Roman* messiah to the Gentiles. Who are the Gentiles? Unsuspecting and ignorant (non-Roman) Europeans who don't know any of the history of the Jews in Israel, except the Catholics will teach that history, and there's not any kind of resources made available to fact-check any of it.

And if one starts poking around, the poison hemlock has been concocted for you.

Yolita, San Francisco, winter, 1951

Chapter 34

Fidel Castro is not repeating the age-old magic words, *translatio imperii*. He brings with him no religion, no royal tradition, doesn't have a name like Charles, Henry, William or George.

This is the problem with Jack Kennedy. He's not following the age-old magic words, *translatio imperii*.

This is *the problem* with Jack Kennedy. He has installed a hotline telephone between Washington DC with Moscow, and these leaders are talking DIRECTLY, bypassing all those other people playing the game of Telephone, otherwise intercepting and transcribing the details.

Now I didn't see this coming back in 1953.

But it's very clear to me now in 1962, the line of succession in this game of Telephone, which was SUPPOSED TO BE Richard Nixon, after Eisenhower, not John F. Kennedy.

The question is not, "Who is running the show?" But, "Who *has been* running the show?" And, "Who STOLE the show?" And, "Who will steal it back?"

This we shall see, won't we?

Chapter 35

This idea of "giving to Caesar," as suggested by Jesus, would have been politically incorrect for his audience, which were Jews, who despised Caesar. The words of Jesus were not written down and distributed during his lifetime; just appreciate that not many people were there at the time Jesus would have said those words.

And those people were long dead, by the time anything Jesus would have said, would have been compiled into a written account, one hundred, two hundred years later. Grant that this story was written in Greek, and not very many people could read Greek, if they could read at all.

So initially, this story was meant for a very select group of people, and not for what Protestants like to call the First Century Church from a common labor class. The texts written in Greek, these were revealed by the Catholics during the FORMATION of the Christian religion. Who did that? We'd like to believe that the whole thing started as a kind of "religion of the common people," but if we notice, it was the formal COUNSELS that made Christianity official.

Who are those people attending the counsels? The bishops, cardinals, the pope, the leaders.

Remember, the Apostle Peter became the first pope, in Rome, because if you were Peter in the period of Tiberius to Nero, Rome is where you'd want to start any kind of new religion, if all roads lead to Rome.

Now the Inca, they don't travel to Spain. Spain would be beyond their imagination. In the same way, no human travels to Heaven. The ordinary, common people, can't imagine Heaven, but the Catholics will explain to them all about it, that Heaven has a kind of "authority" over them, yet a *compassionate* and *benevolent* authority, like what's Catholic, and not like Caesar.

Heaven has GRANTED the Catholic leaders a legal authority, because what rules in Heaven is the Law. The Catholic leaders, they can act like the conquistadors and violate the actual PEOPLE in Peru (assume local land, control belief, educate children, enact strict punishments), and this is okay, why? Because in Peru, there is no higher authority above Spain.

In Spain, there's no higher authority outside of: What's in Heaven, is represented by the Spanish, on Earth, arising through Rome.

This is why Peter must leave Israel, move to Rome, if Rome is the capitol of the empire, then Peter and his heavenly legal authority *trumps* empire; *man's* laws versus Divine rule and Law. But if Peter has died and departed, and the empire embraces Peter, *the empire* assumes the legal authority of Peter through *translatio imperii*.

For reference, the time which would have passed between the death of Peter and Constantine becoming the Roman emperor, would have been longer than between the American Declaration of Independence till now; these ancient people were set within their own history.

Within the first hundred-years of the foundation of the American presidency, a problem arises. Suddenly, there are TWO presidents. One is named Abraham Lincoln and the other is named Jefferson Davis. Jefferson Davis claims that Lincoln is president of only HALF of America, and that HE is the president of the other half (the South).

This would be why, within the foundations of 300 years of the early Christian church, there must be a proper line of SUCCESSION. Which means, for Constantine, in the year 325 or 330 AD, succession runs BACKWARD, the same as with Abraham Lincoln.

For a church to have the authority of Heaven, it must wind backwards somehow to when Heaven came to Earth, granting its authority to a specific line of human authority.

I've gotten ahead of myself. I am not quite as good at lecturing as Thumbert was.

We were discussing Tacitus. Roman historian, 54 to 120 AD.

During his lifetime, there was a SPLIT in the Roman ruling dynasties, with the Julio-Claudian dynasty ending with Nero on one end, and the Flavian dynasty beginning on the other, and each completely different than the other. The Julio-Claudian period begins with Julius Caesar, who ends-up assassinated by his peers. It ends with Nero, who is ordered to commit suicide by the Roman senate. Think of the Julio-Claudians as a Shakespearean dark tragedy.

The Flavians began with a Roman military general named Flavius Vespasian. He is like "a totally great guy," like a Roman version of General George Washington. Vespasian, and those Roman emperors who follow him, begin the tradition of "For the people, by the people." What the common people can SEE with Vespasian, in their Roman government, is the same as what's "actually going on" from the year 69 AD forward and leading to the Five Good Emperors.

As it passes to Constantine, he has a MAJOR PROBLEM. What is it? The Germans. The Romans (with a cultured, highly evolved Mediterranean empire) know that the Germans (uneducated from dark forests) have every intension of destroying Rome and all that it stands for. What does Rome *stand for* according to the Germans? Inequality, top-down tyranny, Caesar.

The Julio-Claudians, set the conflict with Germany in motion, by attacking the North (or the *tribal territories* of what came to be France, Germany, England). One other difference between Rome and Germany, was that northern European women were held in high esteem, while in Rome, not so much.

What mattered also to the ancient Germanic peoples was that no man was placed OVER his peers; their politic was more of a "Knights of the Round Table," based on chivalry.

How do we know this? Tacitus wrote an entire German historical analysis.

The *Flavians*, beginning with Vespasian, predicted a tragedy in the making. The Germans have an old score to settle, and the only way that the Germans will be appeased, is with the entire destruction of the Roman threat.

How do we know this? Because Constantine PREPARES for a pending German invasion. He *moves* the capitol of the Roman empire to where the Germans cannot reach it, to a city which is NAMED after him, Constantinople. He likewise DONATES the entire Western half of the Roman empire to the Catholic church, so when the Germans arrive in Rome, there is no "Rome," just the Vatican City.

Constantine was a busy fellow *or else* he had a lot of help and support from the elite-class.

Anyway, the words of Jesus can now be properly understood: "Render unto Caesar," put down in writing long after Jesus and the Apostle Peter. According to the Flavian dynasty, which encompassed the early Roman Catholic popes to Flavius Constantine, there is NO CAESAR in Rome any more. When you give your empire away to the church, the Roman empire NO LONGER exists. What remains? Just this: "Render unto God what is God's."

How does one "render unto God" after Constantine? By giving to the Catholic church.

The Germans do come down to Rome, unimpeded, sack the city. What do they do after that? They go home. And then, they join the church. What does the church do? It taxes the German people. By what authority? Because, by the authority of Heaven, passed down through Peter, such that, what is rendered unto God, is rendered to Caesar.

This gets cloaked by the church always seeming to be on the edge of bankruptcy; Catholic monks taking vows of poverty and chastity, while the upper-hierarchy is quietly enriched or "in prayer" constantly for the peace of the world. The monks, they get to make wine and beer, and quietly become alcoholics. The nuns also privileged to live in small cubicles, do good, teach, etc.

Some good does come from this form of social system, don't get me wrong.

But this is the question: *Was this religious-politic idea genius or what?*

Yolita, who hated cigarettes
Photo by Jack Parsons, 1952

Chapter 36

Meanwhile, the concepts of egalitarianism: "Everybody is free to make their own decisions," and "We're all equal here," were subverted by Italian-based church hierarchies established all across Europe and Great Britain for about one thousand years.

In 1440, the printing press is invented, and Tacitus is rediscovered, not in Italy, but in Germany. What gains new appreciation in Europe after 1440, is egalitarianism, or "We are all equal here."

Egalitarianism was not originally the idea that "all of humanity is equal," but that the people of YOUR TRIBE are equal. Across Northern Europe, the Catholic church has broken apart tribal identities; by 1517 what replaces Rome are new neighborhood Protestant churches. The dominating theme of each Protestant church is that "we're all equal here, in the eyes of God."

The Roman church can't allow this sort of thing: The resurrection of tribal identities, anti-Roman sentiments, and a rebellion against authority.

Equality is likewise a part of *British* culture (Knights of the Round Table). The British, likewise, are also splintering into local tribal identities apart from the Catholic hierarchy, which fall under the category of Protestant. The PROBLEM becomes, there must be a LEGAL basis for egalitarianism which traces to Heaven's authority, so King Henry VIII announces that he will authorize the new religious egalitarianism as a monarch.

This is a bombshell to what Rome is all about. If you were writing the history of this period in England, and Catholic, you'd nullify Henry VIII's actions by suggesting that the king only wanted to find a way to *divorce his wife*.

The egalitarians will begin to flee Europe in small ships. Each small ship spills onto the shores of the New World forming into individual colonies; all together called New *England*. Certain leaders spill out from these little colonies, who stand for egalitarianism, referred to as Founding Fathers. One of these is Thomas Jefferson, who writes a letter to the British king, stating that the colonies are egalitarian, as Britain is egalitarian, "so understand if the colonies will fight for their own independence from authority, sorry."

No Catholics were allowed within the circle of these Founding Fathers.

The indigenous Native American people already living in tribes across the New World, said to the colonists, "We are also egalitarian." The Founding Fathers replied, "Yes, but you don't trace back to Heaven, so you have no LEGAL BASIS to be here, unless you conform to our *religion*."

If the religious colonizers collected feedback, they could have been interested in what the indigenous people said: "Europeans speak with forked tongue." The Chinese likewise gave this feedback to the original Christian missionaries: "We are not interested in learning more about a God of war."

The official proclamation of the German Empire began at the Palace of Versailles in 1871. Germany named itself "Germany" after Tacitus's book, *Germania*, under the principles of egalitarianism, meaning, "equality amongst people like ourselves." What came to be the Third Reich of the Germans ended with the death of Adolf Hitler, April 30, 1945.

"The Fourth Reich," according to Thumbert, started with "Operation Sunrise" February, 1945, a secret surrender initiated between Allen Dulles (U.S.) and Lieutenant General Karl Wolff (Nazi Germany), which was intended to preserve certain German corporations after the War, and to protect selected Nazi German leaders from prosecution, and to capitalize Nazi losses for American gain, versus Soviet gain.

Allen Dulles, an attorney with the law firm, Sullivan & Cromwell, based in New York City, was given credit for closing its branch office in Berlin during WWII, in protest against Nazi treatment of Jews. However, Sullivan & Cromwell RETAINED its Nazi corporate clients based in Berlin, just moved their *legal representation* to New York (the old shell game).

Allen Dulles then spearheaded a new kind of egalitarianism (equality amongst *people like ourselves*), which was not based upon religious ideals, but upon monied interests of capitalistic corporations. As "colonialism" lost its grip upon indigenous populations following WWII, these Third World nations became vulnerable to further revolutionary uprisings, which could threaten U.S. corporate interests worldwide.

"The Fourth Reich" represented the transfer of Nazi German corporate power-structures to the United States for reimplementation world-wide through law firms, such as Sullivan & Cromwell, with the backing of the U.S. governmental agencies, such as C entral I ntelligence, expanding into new roles under the directorship of Allen Dulles.

One example highlighting "The Fourth Reich" transfer can be observed in the 1962 film, *Lolita*, in which Dr. Zempf, played by Peter Sellers, pretends to be a former "Third Reich" psychiatrist, says to Dr. Humbert Humbert, "We Americans (of the Fourth Reich) ..."

Now please understand, when I heard Thumbert describe in 1952 this transfer of power between Nazi Germany and the United States, I chalked-it-up that he was slightly cynical, recognizing also that Thumbert was born in St. Petersburg.

130

And then, you know, my jaw dropped, when I heard that statement by Dr. Zempf in *Lolita*, this past year, 1962. How in God's name did that line escape *the censors*?

And this is why am writing, that without the lectures of Thumbert, I'd have not seen it. Seen what? Not only is our president, JFK, an Irish Catholic (not English), he is *not* a member of good standing, within the American Fourth Reich, which was launched under Allen Dulles.

For God's sake! He has installed *a hotline* directly between himself and Russia! And he just *fired* Allen Dulles as Director of the C IA. Kennedy has nearly ALIGNED himself with Castro in standing-up to the new imperialism. What I mean is, John F. Kennedy is paying attention to planetary FEEDBACK, and this a serious break in the usual declarations of war, made by "only people like us."

Kennedy fires Dulles, but first pins a medal on him
for service to his country.
The talk around the Agency was that "soon Kennedy
will be returning S. Dakota to the Lakota Sioux."

Chapter 37

How the ancient Julio-Claudian Romans responded to this formidable enemy, the Germans, was to create diplomatic inroads.

One way of doing this, was to offer the sons of Germanic chieftains a FREE EDUCATION in Rome. Sometimes this happened via kidnappings. Which happened to a young German boy, Arminius, taken to Rome and trained, somewhere in time near the year 0 (zero).

In the year 9 AD, Arminius was returned: In the company of a Roman General Varus, who acted as a kind of spy *handler*. Arminius was tasked with meeting with the German tribal leaders to convince them that Rome actually was not ALL BAD. Would the Germans be willing to open trade between empires?

We could suggest that Arminius had been trained in Rome to participate in secret intelligence, and that he was to report to General Varus *intel* about which tribe was where, how many warriors, strengths, weaknesses, etc. General Varus commanded the most elite Roman fighting units, one third of the entire Roman armies, waiting in the wings.

Arminius would be gone on these diplomatic missions to German chieftains for days. What he was actually doing, was acting as a double-agent, providing intel to the Germanic leaders and bringing them TOGETHER to do battle with General Varus and his Roman troops. Arminius was negotiating the time and place to spring an ambush.

When the time was right, the trap was set. Arminius reported to General Varus that the German warriors were assembling, and that he could catch and surprise them, if the Roman troops took a certain narrow route through the Teutoburg forest. Varus fell for it.

The Battle of Teutoburg Forest-ambush resulted in the Roman army's annihilation. No Roman survivors, one-third of the entire military wiped-out.

This battle was an historical HUB. This resulted in several outcomes. It served to unite the German tribes. It also sent a message back to Rome. It weakened Julio-Claudian power. It bolstered the German spirit. It caused the Roman historian, Tacitus, to write an entire book about who the Germans were as powerful egalitarians, titled, *Germania*.

In 69 AD, the Roman general, Vespasian, became emperor. He has been extremely successful leading battles against the Celts in England and quelling rebellion in Israel, but the Germans, he leaves alone.

Vespasian seemed interested in learning more about the religion of the Jews, brings a Jewish scholar from Israel back with him to Rome, named Josephus. Josephus takes on the name of Vespasian, Flavius Josephus. The name *Flavius* is another kind of HUB, as mentioned.

If we look at a map of the Roman empire at the time of Vespasian, the territory is not easily managed as it extends long distances around the Mediterranean Sea, comprised of multiple religions. Vespasian floats the idea of creating a unifying Roman religion after battling the Druids to the North and the Jews to the East, and everything in between; having also spent time in Egypt, observing the impact of their deities upon the culture and a potential rebellion.

The populations residing where we live today have been educated to think of "Rome" as "a brute force, disciplined, war machine;" never does it cross our mind, that prior to the rise of Christianity, that a Roman general would have an interest in *the impact of deities* on a culture.

It would be somewhat RADICAL to imagine a lightbulb turning-on within an ancient Roman general's head, that religion could have a military impact on culture. What if an empire could somehow infiltrate a culture's religious belief, what would that look like? Rather than SUPPRESSING diverse cultures, what if all the peoples could unite, get on the same religious page?

It would never cross *our* minds, why, because we're stupid. What if we weren't actually stupid, just certain gears had been stripped-out, which prevented two-plus-two coming together? What if a Roman leader was floating an idea, and rather than implementing his idea as mandate, he took the time to ask for broader FEEDBACK?

Such as, "Are the people under my rule actually benefitting? Is war stupid or what?"

What if "feedback" could form into a kind of "people's spirituality"? Like how could we have them willingly beat their swords into plowshares?

And make an offer, such that the common people could own their own faith, as much as they could own their own land or have a say in their government. And what if the person in charge, such as Vespasian, was actually astute, recognized that such things TAKE TIME, which are the matters of the HEART, something which anybody is willing to enthusiastically fight for?

Because matters of the heart can't be mandated.

Northern Europe will never come-up with this idea of a lightbulb going off, because Northern Europe has been cut-off from the generous flow of IDEAS, which have circulated the Mediterranean Sea for hundreds, maybe thousands of years. Rome in Vespasian's period was a certain lucky city on a hill, the culmination of Italy itself, jutting into the Mediterranean.

What if the Romans themselves were OVER the Julio-Claudian-type of ruling-style and were ripe for something more forthright? More honoring of the people, for the people, by the people?

What if this new thing could blow the people's minds with delight as they first heard about it?

It would incorporate everything subtle and complex, documenting the evolution of humanity, a culmination, yet simple enough that any peasant could understand, make it their own. What if this new idea could turn, even an established religion, against itself?

And what if, the idea itself was so entirely innovative, that the person who had invented the idea, recognized that this invention could not happen within a single person's lifetime. So the only option was to launch a kind of vision, just a thought, to be carried forward by the next generations, for example, from 79 AD to 325 AD? Then, *muddle the history*.

In fact, it would be so wonderfully extreme and contrary to everything which we thought we knew, the mind would REJECT the new religion as too simple. It would have such transformative power, that "the *world*, the devil, the Caesar's" would reject it, and seek to stop this new religion cold.

Yet our minds can't put two-and-two together. We could never put ourselves into the shoes of a ruler such as Vespasian, without correlating Roman rule to Julius Caesar, the kind of ruler Caesar was, or Nero, pure evil. Thus, when we think of Rome, the mind mostly goes blank.

No lightbulbs are going to turn-on in *our* minds!

Photoshoot, California, 1952

Chapter 38

What happens next is that the Italians destroy every copy of the book *Germania* that they can find, plus a lot of other books, books which might counter the new "unity and universality."

The Romans couldn't afford to remind the Germans of the Battle of Teutoburg Forest or the sacking of Rome beginning in 410 AD. This history is swept under the rug.

Skip forward to 1425 AD. When a single copy of *Germania* is discovered in the Hersfeld Abbey in Germany. The word "Germany" was not used by the Germans, but soon, it will be.

Why?

In 1440 AD, the Germans invent the printing press. Tacitus is so complimentary of the Germanic peoples in his 98 AD book that suddenly everyone across Northern Europe is discussing *Germania*.

Except there's a big problem here, isn't there? What is it? *Translatio imperii.*

The royal families across Northern and Central Europe (and Great Britain) have received authenticity from being grafted into the AUTHORITY of the Catholic religion. There's not *another* lineage which traces back to Jesus higher than the Apostle Peter and the popes.

How can Germany escape the church, yet reclaim its glorious anti-Roman past?

The only way OUT is to disown Flavius Constantine. Instead of THANKING him for his great donation of the Roman empire to the Catholic church, he could be BLAMED for "assimilating" the "First

Century Church" and *spoiling* it. Whatever it was, the Germans could claim that they weren't REWRITING history by abandoning Roman Catholicism, but CLAIMING history.

By 1517 AD, all that the Germans needed was a theological principle onto which they could hang their hat, to get out from under this scourge of rending *unto Caesar*. Boom! Martin Luther and his 95 Thesis pounded to the Wittenberg door. The justification to drop the Catholics was that Jesus IS the ONE and only intermediary between humanity and God the Father, and that no other intermediary, such as Peter, is required. This spiritual law underpins a grafting of a new *political* law.

The Protestants are born.

What does this open? It opens the door for every Northern European monarchy aligned to the Catholic church to abandon ship. Except, this does not happen. Why? Timing. This religious revolution is exploding simultaneous to the birth of *colonialism*.

In other words, there are not many ATHEISTS to be found in Europe during the Sixteenth Century because BELIEF has been hitched to a whole new horse: The uttermost parts.

Once again, history takes a turn towards the stupid.

Chapter 39

I've heard it stated that Goebbels was just as liable for the war, as Hitler, that the Germans were sold many lies, which the foolish citizens bought. Oh no! Goebbels and Hitler believed in the propaganda too. The war did not begin in September, 1939. Oh no!

The wars began in 1425 when a copy of *Germania* was discovered in an Abbey.

The Great War began *not* in 1939, but in the year 9 AD, caused by a single act of a double-cross along a narrow route through the Teutoburg Forest.

This is the hub from which the spokes of time emanate, when the ball of two-thousand years gets rolling. The Protestants and the Catholics represent the spokes, which lead back to Arminius, and not directly to Peter, who may or may not have been fictional.

The Protestants follow their own historical line to *Arminius,* the traitor of the Romans; *Catholics* link to Peter, the endorsement of the Romans.

Peter is not quite as *revered* by the Protestants, and now we know why; the Protestants trace themselves to Arminius, in THEME. While really, truth be told, the Protestants *and* the Catholics trace to *Vespasian*, the one Super-influence, which cannot be easily seen.

Chapter 40

Adolf Hitler.

Ever hear of him? Little known, at the time of his death, he was the *wealthiest* man in Europe.

When he wasn't making speeches, he was making DEALS.

Adolf Hitler was the ultimate profiteer of war.

Every time, even the image of his face was used, and distributed, Hitler was making a nickel. When his image appeared on the postage stamp, Hitler was earning a royalty. The pictures we've all seen of the many train cars loaded with Jews, and other prisoners? Stripped of their possessions, their bank accounts, real estate, gold fillings in their teeth. Did those possessions just disappear?

Whole countries taken over by force, banks emptied of their vaults, museums of their art.

Here's the question: Was Hitler a freak dictatorial anathema or did he create *a pattern* for future politicians to follow?

I.G. Farben.

Ever hear of it? Second-richest corporation in the world at the end of World War II. Formed in 1925, in Germany, a merger of six chemical companies. Started out making dyes. One particularly popular color was *indigo*, made from the Indigofera plant, when a German chemist discovered how to create indigo from coal, which was cheap to produce, making the color *blue* highly profitable.

Germany was rich in coal, as raw materials go. The question became, for chemical companies operating in Germany, "What else can be synthesized from coal?"

Bayer aspirin?

Bayer was a subsidiary of I.G. Farben, started *using coal* to create aspirin. IG Farbin chemists were creating all kinds of amazing new products using coal, including super durable rubber.

IG Farben was also experimenting with the most efficient business models to structure their operations, while between 1925 and 1945, a period which was perhaps the rockiest, most extreme, crazy times to be conducting business in Germany, coming through the worst depression ever, then the rise of fascism. Things could have gone very badly for IG Farben, but instead, the militarization of Germany turned out to be extremely lucrative for chemical (and pharmaceutical and dye) manufacturers.

During WWII, IG Farben employed 330,000 workers. Most of the German men were conscripted into the military, so there was a labor shortage. And, if your factory was part of the military-industrial complex, it will likely be bombed by the enemy.

One way to solve this, would be to move the factories to parts of Germany where enemy bombers couldn't reach, more towards Poland, where coincidentally, there were concentration camps, housing lots of prisoners with not much to do with their time. In 1943, half of the 330,000 IG Farben workers were "slave laborers" who worked really hard or else they'd be sent to the gas chambers. The *poison gas* was manufactured by IG Farben, too.

The labor wasn't FREE. No, IG Farben had to PAY the prisons for each laborer because the Nazi Hitler-owned prisons had COSTS for food and housing the slaves. The problem was that many of the laborers were dying, so they needed to be REPLACED, thus there was true incentive to keep the trains filled with more and more workers.

One IG Farben subsidiary was in the business of processing GOLD and silver, five metric tons of gold and one-hundred tons of silver, processed over the war-period, some of that pulled from the teeth of slave laborers, so as stated previously, it was an extremely efficient business model. Your workers die, you pull out their teeth, check for silver and gold.

Plus, the concentration camps provided prisoners on which to test new IG Farben medicines, many of which proved to be extremely harmful to the patient.

At some point, the tide was turning in the war, and many of the German leaders KNEW IT. What was on their minds? Protecting their own interests. The final year of the war, it was extremely DANGEROUS to be Hitler, because *if* he was "out of the picture," a few select Germans were willing *to surrender* before the Allies bombed their corporations into oblivion.

The Americans, the British (plus Canadians, Australians, etc.), and the French, in early 1945, they were closing-in on Berlin from the WEST. The Russians, closing-in on Berlin from the EAST. Each side had one objective: Collect the spoils of war.

One difference between the West side and the East side, was that the Germans were responsible for 27 million Russian deaths; one quarter of the people from the Soviet Union were either wounded or killed. They're pissed! Plus, the Germans did little *business* with the Russians before or during the war.

The West had *all kinds* of business dealings with Nazi Germany to preserve.

IG Farben had grown to be Germany's largest corporation during the war years, but as mentioned, its factories were about to be bombed into oblivion if the war continued, and certainly, no German wanted to surrender to THE RUSSIANS.

Earlier, I had mentioned the Dulles brothers, Allen and John Foster. They both worked at Sullivan & Cromwell, which legally represented: IG Farben.

Where was Allen Dulles working for the U.S. government as things were falling apart in Nazi Germany? In Switzerland. What was he doing there? He was negotiating for Germany's surrender with Nazi leaders behind Hitler's back. Amazing! A hero! Wasn't *surrender* a good thing?

The Allies included America (West) and Russia (East), who at this time were working TOGETHER. That's Franklin Roosevelt *and* Joseph Stalin. Part of the deal Roosevelt and Stalin had made was that *all deals* made with post-war Nazi Germany were to be ABOVE THE TABLE. This would be important because all sides must *trust* each other in the distribution of war spoils.

Stalin found out, what Allen Dulles was doing in Switzerland, attempting to secretly broker a German surrender WITHOUT the Russians. Stalin was furious. And then Roosevelt would not be happy either, nor would President Truman have forgotten "this blunder" made by the OSS, which was to *get caught*.

Why would Allen Dulles take such risk? The only possible benefit to him, from using his position within the U.S. government, was to benefit Germany's largest corporation, i.e. IG Farben, now a Nazi war criminal-corporation, but also *a client* of the law firm, Sullivan & Cromwell.

On the back of this photo was written:
"I told her to fix her skirt or I'd snap the photo—Marjorie."
"Just smile for the camera!"
California, 1952

Chapter 41

What does this have to do with John F. Kennedy in 1962?

After the War, Allen Dulles returned to his law practice at Sullivan & Cromwell. Harry Truman becomes president at this time in 1945.

John Foster Dulles and Allen Dulles have a keen interest in government. Why? Many of the clients at Sullivan & Cromwell are *international* corporations, such as IG Farben, Standard Oil, and United Fruit. In many ways, the law firm can better serve *their clients*, because the Dulles brothers work IN government.

So, what would be the thing to do in 1952, if you were them? You'd place a bet. You will put all your money on one political candidate. And who is that? Dwight D. Eisenhower.

How does Eisenhower show his gratitude after winning the election? He makes John Foster Dulles the Secretary of State. He makes Allen Dulles head of the C IA. They won their bet.

Could the stars line-up more?

Having land disputes in Guatemala? The Iranians not treating you right? Call the Dulles brothers.

What *problems* in Guatemala? If you were United Fruit growing bananas in Guatemala, which are SUPER CHEAP to grow and harvest, and United Fruit owned ninety-percent of all farmland in Guatemala, you wouldn't want ANY glitches, especially if a "democratically elected" president in Guatemala was nationalizing *United Fruit's* farmland and GIVING it back to the peasants.

Now if you were working at Sullivan & Cromwell, you could pick up the phone, and call someone you knew who worked in government, for example, the C IA. The C IA, with unlimited, secret funding, could somehow TOPPLE that (communist) government in Guatemala, stop this land-giveaway, replace the leadership with anybody United Fruit wanted.

Or if this happened in Iran. If you worked at Sullivan & Cromwell, and your client was Standard Oil, and you didn't LIKE how the government of Iran was reconsidering what "their petroleum resources" were worth, you could pick up the phone. Topple that government.

Now *Standard Oil* chooses who is running Iran. If there's blowback in Iran, that can be fixed one day in the future.

And on it goes! It might be a very *strange coincidence* that all the international clients at Sullivan & Cromwell have a friend in the government.

What about Cuba? What if U.S. corporations had invested heavily in Cuba, while Allen Dulles was the head of the C IA? Those corporations could do pretty much whatever they wanted in Cuba, certainly would want to snuff-out any talk of LABOR UNIONS or the nationalization of farmland. What if some leader stole control, in Cuba, started talking REFORM? Somebody would pick up the phone, call *somebody* they knew in government.

What if *somebody* had EIGHT YEARS to build-out a kind of subversive International SPY infrastructure, which could topple *any* government anywhere, beneath a kind of complacent "do whatever you want" president, like a President Eisenhower? What could anybody do to stop the C IA? You'd BE the U.S. governmental policy, if you ran the C IA.

Unless something happened, which shouldn't have happened. Like you put all your money on the vice president under Eisenhower, Richard Nixon, a similar kind of malleable individual. Then you *lose* that bet? John F. Kennedy wins the election instead? Non-malleable. And Kennedy is in his prime (check out his wife, Jackie!), and you're old, and you're wondering if your best days aren't behind you?

You're Old World Anglo-Saxon Protestant Fourth Reich establishing itself in America.

Kennedy comes into office, not long later fires Allen Dulles.

Kennedy says he will "scatter the C IA to the four winds."

I'm not sure I'd be saying that. I'd go easy on that guy who is named after the airport of the government's capitol.

Chapter 42

One of my favorite lectures given by Thumbert was titled, The Noble Savage.

Whatever I might recount here pales compared to sitting in a recliner next to him, lights low, aromatic wafts of tobacco hanging in the air, the finest bourbon poured over fresh ice in my glass, the tone, the intonations of his voice, the occasional glance from him in my direction.

You see, Thumbert was fascinated by the topic of the noble savage.

He wanted to know: Was there ever a race of noble men and women who lived on this planet, because if there were, he wanted to find them. A man of Thumbert's insight, he would have been quick to draw a conclusion.

Thumbert wouldn't just drone on for no reason. There was a method to his madness, in the same way IG Farben had their own method, as Hitler had a method, which is to conduct business in plain sight. Thumbert wanted to always know, what was beneath, what was hidden, and was there ever "a noble savage?"

By "savage," he meant, *planetary indigenous*. By indigenous, he meant, "whatever was the mind of the peoples untouched by the Industrial Revolution." In Europe, indigenous meant "the mind of the people prior to *translatio imperii* and the very first popes."

Of course, in the U.S., the indigenous would be the American Indian. Thumbert said, "We can't find the American Indian untouched by the Europeans to appreciate what they were thinking."

He said, "We can't find a single Cherokee unmolested by Andrew Jackson or Ponce de Leon."

"If we turn to Africa," he said, "We can't find a single African untouched by Dr. Livingston, because as soon as the savage learns of the white man, the savage African's mind is forever blown."

He said, "What we know of the noble savage is made available through interpretation of how the West sees them."

"Thus, we can admire a man like Sitting Bull, making a stand against his colonizers," Thumbert explained, "Except we only see him through the eyes of General Custer, that it is *Custer* who is making *his* last stand."

Thumbert said that he was forced to give up searching for the mind of the noble savage, until he saw it in an instant, after attending a lecture on astronomy, how astronomers were using telescopes to find distant things from observing the *influence* of a thing, and not the thing itself.

He said that whoever it was, who wrote the Gospels of Jesus, understood this, and we don't care who wrote the gospels, he said. What was so unique about these stories, is that we experience no DISCOMFORT when hearing them, because Jesus can be seen, hence "God" can be seen, through the eyes of the oppressors. We see Jesus through the eyes of Caesar, through the eyes of Pontius Pilate, and Herod, through the eyes of the Jewish establishment.

Can we sympathize? That here is God in the form of a humble man, right in the faces of every established authority, not seen by them. While *we* see him. We wonder how *they* don't see Him. This IS the light, then, which blinded the Apostle Paul, because it was a realization, of something not seen, and suddenly you see it, and *Saul* becomes Paul.

"What did Saul see?" Thumbert asked me, leaning forward, tapping his pipe, checking to see if I had fallen asleep, because I had! So I roused, and he asked me again, "What did Saul *see*?"

Oh God! I was like the kid in school who has fallen asleep, and the teacher has called upon him with a question to answer, except Thumbert is not judging me, he simply said, "He saw the noble savage within himself."

"So," he concluded, "This is an opportunity and a rare one at that. I too can see the noble savage, and yes, when you see it, it blinds you. But if it *doesn't* blind you, then religion is merely a confession, and if it's merely a confession, you're on the other side of it, and what's on the other side of it, Johnny?"

Oh God! He's tapping his pipe, leaning forward, looking at me again, when he says, "Caesar."

"And this is why Jesus says, 'Render unto Caesar what is Caesar's and render up to God what is God's.'"

"Except they don't tell us what belongs to God, do they? You are FORCED to find it all on your own! Because it's not *out there*, is it? It's *in* here," Thumbert said, tapping his chest. "And this is what was seen by the Apostle Paul, that the noble savage was in *him*. Once we see it in ourselves, we can stop the persecution of others, and salute others from what we see, as the Jesus-nobility alive in every other humble living-person."

"Paul must abandon the religious hierarchy of persecution to become his most noble self."

"I don't know why?" Thumbert said, "The story of Paul is diluted as a salvation story about overthrowing the evils of *Adam and Eve*, which further diminishes the power of the self."

He said, "When you see the acceptance Jesus has for others, you lose the fear of the Father. When you lose the fear of the Father, you lose the fear of *translatio imperii*."

"When you lose the fear of *translatio imperii*, you lose the fear of becoming yourself."

Chapter 43

What happened, and you certainly couldn't see it, but Thumbert was turning me into a Christian. He surely assumed that I was his HANDLER, but he was turning it against me, teaching me to see.

As I said, once you can SEE, you can't turn off the seeing.

Chapter 44

I was trying to explain all this to a friend within the Agency, my buddy in Chicago, Kenneth.

I was explaining Cuba and the missile crisis because he wasn't understanding the basics.

I said, "Kenneth, the wheels are turning, can't you tell?"

He wasn't sure. I asked him, what are *wheels* within history? What are the hubs, and what would the spokes look like in today's Cuba? Castro, Kenny! Castro was simply a person who rebelled against the particular influence of *an earlier hub,* and that hub's extending American social design into the Caribbean, but Kenneth wasn't too sure.

It's one man, the revolutionary Castro, rudely defying the Anglo-Saxon horde. He is saying *no* to the sweep of a supposed superior-breed of Europeans. He is saying *no* to the very essential tenets of subjection by the established hierarchy set in motion from events hundreds of years prior on the European continent, questioning, "What does *that* have to do with *this*?"

I asked him, "Can't you understand the basic configurations? I mean, *how long* has this been going on? *What's the frequency,* Kenneth?"

But *you the reader* understand, what Kenny can't see, don't you?

Chapter 45

Kenneth is no fan of Lyndon B. Johnson, in the same way that I am no fan of Allen Dulles.

My opinion of Johnson was that he counter-balanced the Kennedy ticket of the Harvard blue-blood with the raw cowboy spirit of Texas. I likewise admired the combination of Jackie Bouvier with Lady Bird, both super-loyalists to their respective husbands.

I confess that I knew little concerning the executive branch because I had come-up through government through the OSS. Naturally, I would be more aware of recent Cuban events than Kenneth, who was acting as a liaison coordinating intel between the C I A and the S ecret Service, based out of Chicago and frequently in DC.

The nature of our work is piece-work. Each job performs a specific function. The intelligence feeds only upward. At my level, and at Kenneth's level, we never see the bigger picture. Anybody who starts seeing the bigger picture, pretty soon gets a transfer. Not knowing who to trust, and having no benefit to knowing more than we should, we generally keep things to ourselves.

But I've known Kenneth eleven years now, since 1951. His sister attended Marquette College in Wisconsin, as did my sister, lived in the same dorm.

Anyway, when Lyndon Johnson's sister, Josefa, died from a brain hemorrhage last year, I mentioned it to Kenneth, who looked at me with one raised eyebrow, said nothing.

A few weeks later, Kenneth brought it up, at a bar in Oak Park.

He said, while lighting a cigarette, "You know what they say, 'Loose lips sink ships,' well, Josefa Johnson was loose in more ways than one."

I said, "Interesting ... huh, no kidding?"

Kenneth exhaled blue smoke, said, "Oh yeahhh."

"I wouldn't think that would be a particularly wise move."

"Brain hemorrhage? No autopsy? Classic *Texas*."

"Mmmm."

"If I showed you Johnson's file, you'd shit, John, and I mean, shit."

Now Kenneth knows I'm not going to "pick his brain," that would not be *esprit de corp*.

Let's just say that Kenneth divulged no details, and such matters, although private, are *common* knowledge within certain circles. It was through somebody else, who had no clue I was privy to this one detail, the "brain hemorrhage no-autopsy" thing, that "certain others" in Texas had met with "premature passing," tied to a man named Mac Wallace, who worked for Johnson.

Once you get A NAME, you can pretty much learn anything on your own from there.

Like I flew to Nuremburg in 1946 to assist General Donovan with filing information regarding war criminals, sat-in on an interview in process with a Nazi SS sergeant named Shultz, who answered each question with, "I know *noth*ing," then proceeded to offer *every detail*.

Mac Wallace was estranged from his wife, when Wallace found-out she was having an affair with a man named Kinser. Wallace went to the clubhouse of a golf course which Kinser operated, shot him dead with a pistol. Witnesses saw Wallace, took down his car's license plate number, and shortly thereafter, he was arrested fleeing the scene, wearing a torn and bloodied shirt. He's guilty.

Wallace was represented at the trial by John Cofer, longtime attorney to Lyndon Johnson, who had also represented Johnson against voter fraud in his 1948 Senate election. The jury returned a guilty verdict, sentenced Wallace with five years, which was suspended. Wallace served no time in jail. In other words, Wallace owed Johnson a few favors.

Ten years later, 1961, in Texas, an official with the Department of Agriculture, Henry Marshall, was investigating a man named Billie Sol Estes for fraud tied to schemes to fund a political slush fund run by Lyndon Johnson. Marshall turned up dead, ruled a suicide, shot three times with a bag over his head and a hose leading to the tailpipe of Marshall's truck.

Mac Wallace, by coincidence, was working for the U.S. Department of Agriculture, with ties to Billie Sol Estes *and* Johnson, when he shot Kinser in 1951.

Now, enter Robert F. Kennedy, the Attorney General serving under his brother, also JFK's campaign manager. Leading-up to the 1960 election, JFK and Bobby had decided on Governor Symington of Maryland as running mate. However, after a private meeting between Speaker of the House, Sam Rayburn, a Texan, Lyndon Johnson, and JFK, *Johnson* suddenly became the choice for Vice President.

From my intel, which was not difficult to find, J. Edgar Hoover had already taken steps to have Jack Kennedy photographed with women in compromised situations, including with a Dutch honeypot spy, and including medical records detailing JFK's many medical impairments. By coincidence, J. Edgar Hoover and Lyndon Johnson were *next-door* neighbors in Washington DC. You can't make this up!

And by coincidence, Kennedy is known today to want to force Hoover into retirement soon in 1964, while Johnson, supports Hoover's *continued* service as Chief of the F BI.

This does match the severe acrimony between Bobby Kennedy and Johnson.

And it does match something J. Edgar Hoover might do; have pictures taken.

It matches the rumors that Bobby Kennedy has been investigating the Billie Sol Estes and Lyndon Johnson ties to massive fraud, which the F BI refuses to look into, and yet, will likely result in an indictment of Johnson, not just the ending of his political career, but jail time.

Johnson with Bobby and Jack

And it matches with the serial marital affairs of Jack Kennedy, already legendary.

And nobody is pointing fingers, but LBJ is also quite notorious for his serial marital affairs. And his love for scotch, which I'd know, through a friend with the Secret Service, whose job it is to make sure that cases of scotch travel everywhere the Vice President travels as a highly functional alcoholic who can chain-smoke three packs a day.

Lesser known, was that LBJ's sister, Josefa, was "quite close" to Mac Wallace. Remember him? The Department of Agriculture exec and the possible "murderer" of Henry Marshall to prevent him from going public in 1961. You know, "Loose lips sink ships."

Now if Josefa Johnson had loose lips, while sleeping with Wallace, that wouldn't be good for LBJ.

Who stands to benefit, if only half of this is true, and Kennedy suddenly experiences a massive *aneurism*, too? Wouldn't that be a huge surprise?

One thing I do know. If anything does happen to Kennedy, Johnson has a very small window to make it happen, given Bobby Kennedy's proactivity with his brother's upcoming 1964 campaign. And it's not like America hasn't had presidential assassinations. My bet is that Johnson couldn't withstand scrutiny, but here is the problem with that: The Communists. ·

Who's going to take-out the leader of the Free World, with short-range Russian nuclear missiles pointing at DC? There's just too much coordination involved to pull off a coup, in the middle of a tense conflict with Russia.

Did LBJ have the upper hand?
What we are looking at is Kennedy, war hero,
and Johnson, given a medal, fake war hero.

Chapter 46

After the founding of America, John Quincy Adams and James Monroe decided that colonization of North America is OVER. This is called "The Monroe Doctrine." That means, *Europe is to keep its hands-off* further colonization efforts of BOTH North and South America, and in return, America will stay out of Europe's business.

France and Spain laugh, but Britain doesn't. Britain agrees to help ENFORCE the Monroe Doctrine, while America begins to build a Navy. The Monroe Doctrine includes all the Caribbean islands, including Cuba.

The map of the planet at this time appeared something like a board game. A few key players dominated the game. There are very few places by the year 1800 remaining free from colonization, but some of these places include China and Japan, nations which have been traditionally allied with Hawaii and Korea.

These "Oriental" nations have formed a centuries old pact similar to "The Monroe Doctrine." Together they are stronger to defend against encroachment by white Europeans.

Meanwhile, Hawaii falls. And Korea forms a treaty-alliance with America. But Japan and China are defending their right to keep foreigners out.

China and Great Britain will conduct trade. England produces nothing China wants, while the English want Chinese products such as tea, spices, dishes, and silk. The Brits can purchase these items, but only with the precious metal, silver. What happens? England loses its valuable silver stockpiles.

Because England controls India, opium can be smuggled into China through India. Opium is purchased on the black market in

China only *with silver*. Hence, not only does Queen Victoria get her silver back, but the entrepreneurs hatching this scheme grow extremely wealthy themselves, as do a few select American families, including the Delano's, as in Franklin Delano Roosevelt.

Opium is serving to weaken Chinese society and the Chinese emperor begins to open communications with Queen Victoria to reign-in these British opium smuggling operations. Upon the receipt of *silence* from the queen, China declares war on Great Britain. The First Opium War began in 1839, lasted three years. The second, 1856 to 1860. China lost.

One result was that Hong Kong was ceded to Britain. The other was that various ports were forced open for future trading between the two nations.   However, the REAL PRIZE amongst European nations was to capture ALL OF CHINA for itself.

Now America has The Monroe Doctrine, but this refers to Europe, nothing ever mentioned regarding exploiting the Far Pacific.

So in 1853, American Commodore Perry sailed four ships into Tokyo Bay to encourage an end to Japanese isolationism by threat of force. This began a long relationship between Japan and the U.S., and mutually beneficial, as Japan militarized.

In other words, the alliance between China, Japan, and Korea was being broken-up piecemeal, China having its own problems with Great Britain.

Japan saw the writing on the wall, was willing to cooperate. Officials there began wearing tall black Abraham-Lincoln stovepipe hats as a sign of solidarity with the U.S. Navy. The U.S. told Japan that it needed a kind of Monroe Doctrine for itself, to protect its own waters, and to *expand*.

Why is this important to know? These are SPOKES, originating from a hub, which is Anglo-Saxon egalitarian (*Germania*) supremacy concepts being proven by European and American colonialism spreading across the globe. The British controlled the seas, while more and more, America was beginning to control the Pacific.

Just as the Inca royalty ceded to the Spanish royalty, so Japan ceded to America, and in return, America deemed Japan *superior* to every other Asian people by the principle of *translatio imperii*. In other words, only a superior Anglo-Saxon-American empire could designate this concept of superiority to another nation, such as Japan.

One way to prove this, according to the American advisors, was for the Japanese to wage war against its neighbor, Korea, while America turned a blind eye. The ultimate goal was for Japan to attack China, too. This strategy would WEAR DOWN Japan, while destroying China, then to negotiate a peace, brokered by the United States in forming new Pacific puppet states.

In the meantime, the U.S. under Theodore Roosevelt would build a canal through Central America at Panama, to control future shipping between Asia and Europe.

All this was happening according to plan, except for one minor small detail: Mao Zedong.

The Americans had already installed its own dictator in the Republic of China, Chiang Kia-shek. The Chinese people themselves saw this incursion, raised-up their own defense, called "The People's Army." From here, we know the rest of the story. Including that Japan was somewhat busy bombing the Chinese, when the U.S. government was forced to stop supporting Japan's war effort, forcing Japan to bomb the U.S. Seventh fleet at Pearl Harbor, so Japan could attack Indonesia for oil and gain the resources formerly supplied by Franklin D. Roosevelt.

I realize this is oversimplified, but I'm not writing the entire history of the world.

Anyway, if the U.S. had been given the opportunity to just BUY China, America would have, in the same way it was able to PURCHASE Puerto Rico, Guam, the Philippines, from Spain.

Cuba was purchased in a variety of smaller transactions of American investment, held privately, until Fidel Castro took control in 1959, kicked out the Americans, nationalized land and all the outside U.S. investments previously made into Cuba.

What principle was Fidel Castro violating? The Monroe Doctrine. He was deemed as technically an OUTSIDER coming in and taking over a country within AMERICAN waters. In other words, the Cubans technically didn't own anything about their own island.

So this wasn't going to fly.

Now what?

General Dwight Eisenhower was president. He was fully supportive of the C IA, at first, because the C IA's mission had been presented to him like this: Why go to WAR with rogue anti-American enemies, if you could covertly get in behind the lines, *assassinate* the radical leader, instead?

Fewer American soldiers are involved/risked/killed/wounded under this covert model.

With the case of Cuba, The Monroe Doctrine could be enforced by the C IA, not the military. All kinds of crazy schemes were designed by Allen Dulles and the C IA to quietly take Castro out, including using the C IA's Mafia connections in Cuba.

None of these schemes worked.

What happens next? Richard Nixon, Eisenhower's vice president, was supposed to win the 1960 election, totally upset by Joseph, Bobby, and Jack Kennedy.

Enter Nikita Khrushchev, the General Secretary of the Communist Party of the Soviet Union.

Fidel Castro, knowing full well that he has been the target of multiple assassination attempts made by the C IA, turns to Khrushchev for help. This would be a drastic violation of The Monroe Doctrine of an encroachment by an hostile country within U.S. waters.

Keep in mind, U.S. plans for China had JUST RECENTLY been thwarted by Mao Zedong in China, and still stinging.

President Kennedy's Joint Chiefs of Staff meet and are unanimous: Invade Cuba with the U.S. military. The proposals included bombing the Island of Cuba out of existence. And if Russia has a problem with that, bomb Russia out of existence.

The ratio of nuclear weapons America had built in 1960 was ten-to-one over Russia: 25,000 warheads compared to about 3,000. The U.S. could fly bombers within reach of every major Russian city, which was called "first strike" capability.

What appealed to Khrushchev about Cuba, was that building nuclear missile sites on the island gave Russia at least some opportunity to balance this power. Plus, the U.S. had placed secret nuclear warheads in Turkey in violation of the U.S.-Soviet nuclear treaties and Khrushchev knew it. Khrushchev was saying, "If you come *here*, we're going there."

Kennedy did not follow the advice of the Joint Chiefs of Staff. He was unwilling to authorize the U.S. military to invade Cuba under any conditions; he still believed in negotiation to balance these imbalances.

It would be no stretch to wonder which insiders were asking, "Who else might replace Kennedy, perhaps slightly more *bloodthirsty*?"

Allen Dulles offered a compromise. The C IA would train a small army of 1,400 Cuban exiles to rise-up against Castro, in what's called "a false flag." By 1961, the C IA had experience with such things. If it worked, Castro would be easily replaced. If it failed, the U.S. military could deny any involvement, like, "Hey, we can't control what the Cubans do."

Kennedy did not like the plan, but had to do SOMETHING. Dulles advised Kennedy that once the Cuban exiles established a bulkhead, that the Cuban military would turn against Castro. It was deceit: The idea that 1,400 C IA-backed ground forces could defeat 25,000 Cuban militia. The Dulles plan was to *force* Kennedy to *draw in* the U.S. military to overthrow Castro.

The *real* plan had not been presented to Kennedy, which had been floated with Eisenhower, to launch an attack with phony anti-Castro revolutionaries WITH SUPPORT from U.S. air and naval forces. The latter component had been left out in Kennedy's briefing.

Things started going badly with this fake revolution in Cuba from the beginning. Kennedy was called upon to authorize air and naval support, but he refused. The Dulles plan therefore failed because Kennedy failed. The C IA was caught with its pants down because Castro took prisoners and they talked. Also, this bolstered the relationship between Castro with the Cuban populace, and between Castro with Khrushchev.

And none of it would have happened if Kennedy had just followed the advice from his Joint Chiefs of Staff. Kennedy went rogue on the establishment (and look at the result). If *Nixon* had won the election, Cuba would already have been toast.

Chapter 47

Then, you know, Kennedy goes on television telling the American people to consider building BOMB SHELTERS in their own back yards. With a nuclear advantage of ten-to-one, the Joint Chiefs of Staff can't believe that the Americans are being subjected to Secondary Status in front of the entire world.

Plus, Kennedy FIRES Dulles, and other directors, from the C IA. Kennedy states publicly that he wants to DISMANTLE the C IA. Kennedy is taking down Lyndon Johnson and slating J. Edgar Hoover to retire. And remember that Joseph Kennedy, the father, had advocated for appeasing Hitler, and now his son, Jack, is appeasing Khrushchev, which is all on the world stage.

What can be done to show the world, that America is still ruthless?

Not to mention, that Vietnam is in a civil war, that communism is about to topple ANOTHER nation, and Kennedy wants to PULL OUT all U.S. military advisors there. After going through all that trouble of entering WWII, sacrificing, winning, certain Americans were watching Kennedy, throwing it all away.

Plus, there is a swimming pool beneath the White House and Kennedy is organizing swimming parties with young female interns down in that pool.

While crisis is in full swing, Kennedy is swinging, too. We know, because the Secret Service is following his every move, and to the Joint Chiefs of staff, things are just *out of control*. Johnson is likewise out of control, so in my mind, this protected Kennedy, but now, I think not so much; Johnson is proving himself *ruthless*, I mean. It's already on his resume.

As Thumbert would have said, "Who stands to gain in the shit-show since time immemorial?"

Chapter 48

One final piece to this puzzle, is Allen Dulles, IG Farben, and the American business model, which is what they don't teach you at Harvard Business School.

That is, a business is highly profitable if it can solve a problem, such as making a headache go away.

But that same business is *exponentially* profitable if it can likewise be *causing* headaches. In this case, you'd put your chemists to work. To find the chemicals which *cause* a headache and start manufacturing those, while manufacturing aspirin.

What if IG Farben, or Bayer, is in the chemical business or in pharmaceuticals or farm fertilizers and weed killers? Now if you also sell soaps, or foods, you insert the chemical into the ingredients which coincidentally causes a headache, absorbed through the skin or through the nose. Then, you sell aspirin.

Technically not, just as an example, that the model is to avoid governmental regulation or detection.

How this is done, if anybody were to consider it, would be to donate large sums of the profits to the highest educational institutions, to ENDORSE the safety of your soap, pill, or spray: "This new thing is a MIRACLE!"

When customers begin to notice these products give them "headaches," the company has already conducted in-depth medical studies, again, proving the safety, because there could be many other causes of a headache, not your products.

Or a medicine ITSELF could cause a side-effect, which *another* of your medications will treat. It's the concept of buying low, selling high, then selling *again* for a guaranteed second sale. How a corporation likewise "buys low," would be, to have your government representatives *subsidize* the development of your particular products.

Once expertise and credential are established and accepted by a base of customers, who else is more qualified to be placed into governmental-bureaucracy oversight than your own executive staff? Through this, the government would take responsibility for the safety of your products; the corporation is set-free from all liability/legal-costs.

This has been described as a revolving door: Also accepted by a base of customers that the best experts to *regulate* the products sold to the public are the same people who make them.

With the case of IG Farben, it was broken into its various subsidiaries under the watchful eye of its protectors from America, then those German subsidiaries, or "Dr. Zempf," integrated into American society as: *We* Americans.

IG Farben's Bayer Aspirin, they're fully protected, expanding (can't lose!), suddenly growing America's corn, and this would be accepted by a general base of customers. To question anything about it, that's not the American way.

I am well aware that I sound indignant. Sorry, I didn't used to be. And I am not now.

Nobody incarnating into this world was ever meant to become *indignant*.

And that's the other "beauty" of this economic model: All those who see what's truly going on, are more likely to feel indignant. The greater the indignancy, the more likely it becomes, that *these* are the ones, who feel a major headache coming on.

Chapter 49

The business model, if done right, is to arrange the chairs so that there is no difference between government and the business; it's all ONE.

The business, if it builds bombs, can also declare war.

In this case, the Western Allies would NEED the Soviet Union, as motivation to go after the rest of the planet (to save it) from communism. In other words, you already are there to provide the solution to the problem you just created.

In other words, as Kennedy befriends Khrushchev, Kennedy is throwing a wrench into post-War planetary re-colonization efforts of the Fourth Reich Allied Forces: Invade or topple any nation or government who even hinted at nationalization of its land, mineral rights, natural resources, etc., labor rights, etc.

Sullivan & Cromwell, they don't need *Allen Dulles* in the government, just an Allen Dulles clone, the elected officials, the executive branch, etc. Law firms brokered deals between corporations and government to gain former colonized lands, mineral rights, natural resources, etc.

In other words, World War II created a vacuum where many nations were left with no established power-structure following 1945.

Within the vacuum, IG Farben (or IG Farben clones) pick up the telephone. They call Sullivan & Cromwell (or Sullivan & Cromwell clones), who in return, pick up the telephone. On the other end of the line is Allen Dulles (or Allen Dulles clones).

"Adolf Hitler" industrialists, along with their attorneys, get richer, and the rich get richer (or Adolf Hitler clones).

But here's a clue: The homage paid to such *a system*, such as, for all of the possible heroic Americans you could name the capitol's airport after, you'd name it after Dulles. This name is HOMAGE to a kind *of system* of government.

Which is where? In DC. District of Columbia. Another homage. To Columbus.

Colonization. Corn. Corporations. IG Farben. And April 7, 1948, is the start of the IG Farben, Bayer Aspirin sponsored, World Health Organization: WHO. Thumbert told me that the WHO might have a question-mark behind it.

He said, "I'd accept a blanket to keep me warm, but not if Klaus Barbie was giving it away."

I asked Thumbert what he meant by the word *clone*.

He explained that John Wayne is an actor who often plays the role of the unexpected hero. The heroism of the movie character gets transferred upon the person of John Wayne himself. His fans expect this of him; fiction crosses over into what is nonfiction.

Thumbert asked, "What if scientists in white lab coats brought John Wayne into their laboratory to study what it is, which creates the *heroic possibility* within the individual? They won't find it, will they?"

"They shine a light into his eyes, use a magnifying glass, X-ray his skull. The best that they will find is the *clone* of a hero, the actor."

"The man himself, or the woman herself, Joan of Arc, for example, is not the heart that beats, but is found within the soul of the individual which lives *between* the beats; it's the space between the notes, where we feel the symphony."

"Clones cannot *see* the essence of a thing, therefore, cannot appreciate the essence."

"We read in Victor Hugo, *The Last Day of a Condemned Man*, created from a laboratory of the poet's insight, which is very different from the laboratory of science. Our eyes are opened to what lies within the person, the soul, which is precisely what science cannot find, which is that which is the most heroic, yet unseen, right-up until the moment when it's seen."

Anne Frank, just another unseen heroic Jewish girl taking-up precious space at Bergen-Belsen.

"The society of the clone, is the society which advocates conformity under the pretense of 'what's good for all.' This represents the error of society, because what's good for all, is rarely what's right for the soul. Even for those at the top, who believe they have mastered their society, no, it's not right for their souls, either."

The French existentialists saw this, what others were not seeing, which is, what happens to the soul, when we follow any form of science, which exalts the mind of the clone.

Chapter 50

"Is this a purposeful colonization of the American people, now being pushed into the suburbs?" I asked Thumbert, as he sat pensively between puffs on his pipe. "No," he replied, "It's blowback. Absolutely accidental."

Within the Western Protestant King James version of the Christian Bible, the stories are not what they seem to be on the surface. Take the story of Jesus, who sends his disciples in a boat to cross the sea, as a storm buffets their boat, and Jesus appears walking on the water.

We already know the special circumstances under which Jesus was born, or incarnated, granting him special powers. But this is different, because Peter sees Jesus, asks if *he* also can walk upon the water, and Jesus says, "Step out upon the water."

The mystery, is that there is nothing noted regarding Peter's birth as special, and that Jesus had the option to tell Peter, "No Peter, stay in the boat, for you are not born under a star, as I am."

We watch this super-special baby Jesus mature into a person who can walk on water and we are to assume His options and choices will be vastly different from the options we have been given. In other words, nobody is going to play the shell game with Jesus. Yet the devil tries. The devil tells Jesus that Jesus can *rule the world*.

We can notice a kind of contrast between "all who rule the world," with the inside of the person, and God, who incarnated as the humble human, Jesus, walked around, and *rejected* ruling from a human seat of power. Jesus wore dusty sandals, sat on the ground, spit in the dirt. The PROBLEM is that there's not an opening for a leadership position within a corporation which Jesus can fill.

Victor Hugo famously stated, "Nothing is more powerful than an idea whose time has come."

Thus, the gospels, as an idea whose time had come, never show Jesus taking control of organizations. Jesus does not collect followers into a larger organization, rather continually sends them away.

This story of Jesus is put to writing and what might strike us is that only the smallest minority in those ancient days could read.

These stories will be not available to the common people for the next thousand years. So the story of Jesus, was written for the HIGHER classes to be privy.

In other words, one message in the Bible is for how to conduct oneself within one's brief slice of existence. And for how to treat others: With honor and with humility.

When Jesus says to "Render unto Caesar," the story is speaking to the elites. He is telling THEM to render *unto God*; Jesus points towards what is within the HEART. Caesar represents the clone. Jesus represents the inner-quality. At the same time, Jesus represents God in the gospels, if God became human.

God is saying, "Look, if I wanted to make clones, I'd have made clones."

God is essentially communicating to the religious leaders through the gospels, "Stop this cloning of yourselves."

Chapter 51

"What's beautiful about the mother of Jesus, Mary, is her *face*," Thumbert said.

"And, the father's face is beautiful. The faces of the grandparents, also beautiful."

"The baby, Jesus, received every adoration. The authors of this story are telling us how important this is, the faces, because *faces* show-up to look upon the baby."

"The wife, the husband, the sweetheart, the lover, likewise fulfill this role. The role of sexual union involves the body, but more importantly, the face, and every tiny muscle in it."

"The character of the baby Jesus, received adoration, yet we don't see *the drive* for adoration in the grown man. Why not? Jesus stood in relation to *something other*. Which was what? His journey. His relationship to something other, which is not seen by others."

"The devil became attached to the adoration, while Jesus is never attached to it. So, this is the model. What was Jesus attached to? Something greater not seen by anybody else."

"And this is the tragedy of Adolf Hitler, not that he was *evil*, but that he became attached to the adoration."

We see him attempt to salvage his life at the very end," Thumbert pointed out. "He does this by marrying Eva Braun. This is a man who has been humbled, who has fallen from the pinnacle of history, now we see him taking an entirely new course of direction."

"He is showing the rest of the world, that from this day forward, he will do the honorable thing. He will be a man of integrity, a man who will keep his word, as long as they shall live."

"'Ahhh,'" we say, "'Too little, too late.'"

But you have got to start somewhere.

Chapter 52

I'd suggest to skip over this next chapter. And skip the next. I merely include these details as documentation. I myself have no interest in presenting a cosmology. Skip to the notes. Don't wear yourself out. As Thumbert put it, these are footnotes, not your dragons to slay.

I'll never forget the day Jean and I drove Dr. Thumbert from Chicago to Des Moines. As I mentioned, we arrived at night. I wanted Thumbert to get a feel for his new city, so we passed through the downtown. I particularly wanted him to see the impressive Iowa State Capitol building and the Polk County Courthouse. And all of downtown Des Moines.

Iowa State Capitol

Thumbert said, "No, no, this looks like Prague."

Jean said, "I hope that you will feel at home in your new city! Tomorrow we will take you over to Drake, just as impressive as all of Des Moines."

He asked, "And *farmers* built *this*? No, no, this looks like Prague."

Prague? Or downtown Des Moines?

I had not yet appreciated the wheels which were turning within the mind of a Thumbert.

We must recall that Thumbert was born in St. Petersburg, and had lived all across Europe, must have seen Des Moines very differently. Later, after listening to Thumbert's lectures, I came to appreciate his keen interest in architecture, and that he was forming a kind of hypothesis, which he was developing, even in our conversations.

I found many of his ideas preposterous, yet I put all of them into my reports. Sometimes I would see Thumbert taking walks by himself in downtown Des Moines. I know that he took tours inside many of the older buildings, absolutely taken speechless by Terrace Hill, the Governor's Mansion. I had not been inside of it, and Thumbert told me, "The interior is equally as impressive as the exterior, like any *palace* in Europe or Russia, the many kinds of marble, the wood, the carvings, the layouts of the grounds with pools, monoliths, gardens, exactly like Prague, St. Petersburg, Moscow."

The interior of a Des Moines frontier hotel, built by farmers?

I believe he was struck by the contrast of Iowa's architecture with the Old World, how similar it was, that he had always assumed that the great cathedrals and palaces had been built by skilled artisans of the past. He said that he wanted to meet the artisans of Iowa who could build such finery he saw, but he had met not *one* person in Des Moines who had such skills, not a father nor a grandfather who had such skills, but only farmers, he met.

Thumbert said the Old World buildings in Iowa possessed the identical spires, with odd metal shapes projecting into the air, which he called "energy collecting devices." He called it technology, possibly from the Middle Ages, or before that. His suspicion, back in Europe, was that the great cathedrals were actually like great machines which collected energy from the air.

And if this technology had been lost, then other technologies could have been lost, such as methods of propulsion, that you could fly a great ship, with the right technology, fueling itself from the atmosphere itself.

As I said, I reported all of this, which I thought nonsense, yet, I believe this is why Thumbert was sent to meet Jack Parsons for collaboration. I mean, after Thumbert was given access to Hangar Eighteen, spent time in Ohio, studying bizarre spacecraft and propulsion.

One day, Thumbert was extremely excited. I asked him, "What is it?" He sat me down, did not even bother to light his pipe.

He told me, that he learned that "Des Moines" had a meaning. It meant "of the monks." And then, he had an epiphany. I thought this nothing to get excited over. But he asked me, "Where are the MONKS? They are not here. Monks do not build a city such as this and farmers do not build a city such as this. This city was here, for who knows HOW LONG. It was called the City of Monks only because it appeared like a city built by Renaissance artisans."

"Farmers did not build Des Moines," he said.

I could not *wait* to put all of this down into my report.

He told me that in Harold Hayes's old office, was a collection of old books. Amongst his collection were original keepsakes from all the World's Fairs, including books, booklets, flyers, pamphlets, old tickets. From places such as Chicago, San Francisco, St. Louis, and all over the planet, at the turn of the Twentieth Century.

"Why all these World's Fairs?" he asked me. "During an era when international travel was by a slow boat? Or by horse and buggy?"

He said, "It would take many days by horse and buggy just to get from Chicago to St. Louis, even in 1904. Cars? What *roads*?"

He showed me a souvenir book from the St. Louis Fair, flipped through pictures, asked me if I thought the architecture appeared to be temporarily built for a fair, in stone, but what was his point? He said, "No, it was already there standing, built with quarried blocks, and waiting for the pioneers to stumble upon."

I asked him, "*What* was already there?"

He replied, "St. Louis! No different than any buildings you would find in Greece or Italy."

I said, "You are telling me that *St. Louis* is as ancient as Rome? And Des Moines, too?"

"Yes, and why not?"

He said, "The Spanish conquistadors, they asked the Inca, 'Who built all these great cities in Peru?' The Inca replied that the cities were already there. The gods had built them."

Thumbert further explained, "The Inca did not know from where the Spanish had come, so the Spanish must be the gods, who have returned to occupy the old infrastructure which the Inca had settled *around*. The Inca royalty, naturally, were more than willing to put themselves beneath the Spanish, and convert to their religion, because to the Inca, the Spanish were the gods, who had previously built their cities."

"There are neoclassical buildings in Peru, which are exactly the same architecture as in Des Moines, and not built by *monks*," he said. "Forget Machu Picchu, that's from even earlier."

"This planet is like a chalkboard, and we cannot know, how many times it's been erased."

Now Thumbert rarely spoke of his work at Hangar Eighteen, but once he felt obliged, knowing full well I now could not believe a word he had said. He said he had observed the seeming alien spaceship wreckage, that being from a recent crash, but he told me there was not one craft, but many, of all sorts, requiring the entire hangar to house them.

He said, "I told them at Hangar Eighteen, 'These are advanced craft, all of them, except not from our time, because these are *ancient*. Where did you find them?'"

Thumbert explained, "This information was beyond my clearance, and their clearance, so I told them where these crafts were found. 'They were found amidst ancient *ruins* in America, weren't they?'"

"And how did I know?" he continued. "Des Moines. St. Louis. Chicago. Prague. Vienna. The people of Europe were just as dumb as the Inca, just too proud to admit they did not know who had built their cathedrals, their great marble pillars and halls of justice, even the castles, they did not build, but inherited."

"Nor the spacecraft, made from rare metals, craft which had been melted down into the weapons of Europe dating back to Caesar."

"In America, the native tribes, knew full well of such metals, from ancient spacecraft wrecks, but lacked the technology to melt such things to make other things, and here come the pilgrims, to St. Louis, and to Des Moines."

"*This* is what drove Meriwether Lewis insane after his long expedition with Clark: The empty cities, like the ruins of Greece, and a few metal spacecrafts they had discovered in the middle of nowhere, eventually collected, moved into hangars."

"They had no explanation for the ancient structures standing cold in the wilderness any more than archaeologists credibly explain the many hundreds of pyramids found everywhere across the planet. In our minds, Des Moines could not be *ancient ruins*, partly because the buildings appear more recent, but I am telling you, these are ancient. Iowa farmers did not build these."

Thumbert concluded, "I know you look at me as if I am crazy. Haha, it's much easier for you to believe in Christmas, and Easter, Michelangelo, and Queen Victoria!"

"Even the greatest historical hubs to which I refer, connect to a past, invented in its entirety," Thumbert said. "Name me an event from the past, even one of the greatest of hubs, and I'll show you the grand illusion."

"The historical hubs, with spokes, fabrications, too, despite what I've told you."

Thumbert said, "Des Moines, I thank you!"

"Don't look too closely," he said. "If you hope to maintain your sanity."

Chapter 53

Translatio imperii.

Jack Parsons.

One of Thumbert's final lectures.

"Nothing is more important," Thumbert began, "Than an idea whose time has come."

He continued, "What was the great *idea* of Jack Parsons?"

Parsons spent quite a bit of his
limited spare time with Yolita.
After he got funding, the plan was for Y.
to join him and M.C. in Mexico.

"Jack appreciated, as I did, that the most dynamic powers we cannot see. However, one must LOOK FOR it. Or this power is happy to go on unnoticed, or just as equally happy to help and guide the seeker."

"This power is demonstrated by the butterfly; the accidental flapping of its wings is what underpins the academic fields of history, sociology, and physics, not science-method."

"Jack came into this world with all his plumbing and wiring intact, such that he could process new information like turning on a light switch, while flushing distraction and anything superfluous down the drain. Nobody needed to explain to him that the biblical texts weren't written for a person like him, so if he read the gospels, he snuck into the texts, noted that Jesus was practicing *magic*."

"Jack noted that Jesus taught in code, and this code would be missed by the bureaucrats, and that 'practicing magic' was explained by them as the work of the devil. Nobody needed to explain to Jack that the New Testament was written at the height of the Roman Golden Age which opened a CONTEXT to dump every spiritual secret compiled for centuries from around the Mediterranean into one great teacher, or as they said, a God who became human."

"It's almost too embarrassing that these biblical stories were made *historical*: Notice the Star of Bethlehem, the Three Kings, the repetition of the number 12, Moses appears upon the Mount of Transfiguration, the Apocrypha, an evolution of themes, etc."

"If Moses was metaphorical, Jesus is metaphorical, if both appear in each other's stories."

"And, as it's coming to historical and archaeological light, the Israelites could not have been settled in Egypt; meanwhile, for two-thousand-years, nobody had the means to investigate it."

"Jack instantly grasped that Jesus didn't show-up to start a new religion, rather was a compilation and a synthesis. So, across the West, Jesus was misinterpreted as something *new*."

"Then, the Greeks, the Egyptians, the Sumerians have been misinterpreted as *old*, but these civilizations are relatively new, in relation to the chalkboard-planet."

"Jack told me, that if the story of Jesus had been understood as science fiction, drawing upon the very-old mythic symbols and caricatures, the power unleashed through the launch of Christianity could have been ten-fold."

"Constantine distracts you and me," Thumbert said. "This was easy because ancient Northern Europe had been unfamiliar with Greece, Egypt, Mithra, etc.; could not read Latin. The Catholics were as unimaginable to the ancient Germans as the Catholics were unimaginable to the Inca."

"If there was an Apostle Peter in a boat, in a storm, who sees Jesus out walking on the water, he represented the person with 'instinct connected to his gut,' who can put this into words, asks, 'Can I walk on the water?' While the rest of the disciples, their minds didn't even go there; they saw Jesus on the water, didn't think to *ask* if they could step-out of the boat, even after Peter asked."

"So no, Jack heard stories like this, recognized that he was reading a handbook for how to conduct magic, which first of all, is the recognition that the experts will tell you, what *they* believe Jesus was teaching every time. Except, once anybody realizes that the New Testament was written as a compilation for the elites, Jack was determined to break the code."

What I read between the lines, was that Thumbert most likely took LSD with Parsons, to assist the breaking of the codes of magic. Thumbert would have been CURIOUS enough to do it.

"Jack is the only person I've met who can blend modern physics *into* Jesus *into* Thelema," Thumbert said. "His spiritual influences were not distinct from his breakthroughs in rocketry."

186

"Moses became the *magician*," Jack told Thumbert once, "So why shouldn't I?"

"The Catholic church was, in truth, an insider club for those who practiced magic. The wearing of purple slippers indicated their status to each other in magical terms."

"You wear slippers; I wear slippers. You wear strange hats; I wear strange hats."

"Everybody else was following a religion, wore boots, threw each other into the bog."

"The Vatican City did not allow such ruffian non-magical Germanic boot-wearers inside."

"After God created Adam and Eve, and was walking in the garden, He saw that *they* had covered their nakedness; no, God *wanted* them naked or he wouldn't have started the show with them naked; would have dressed them in clothing straight out of the box."

"This is explained very poorly, so when it comes down to the philosopher, Descartes, saying, 'I think, therefore I am,' this throws all the magic into the *brain*, when Descartes could just as easily have stated, 'I am *naked*, therefore I am.'"

"The brain is magic, but so is *the body*; Parsons was not the first to appreciate the wisdom of *the body*."

"The elite-class restricted the human body only to their privilege. Other religious bureaucrats cut a hole in their bedsheets to procreate *between* the sheets. Literally, this is their foreplay, using a scissors to cut a small hole in the covering sheet and then blowing out the candle."

"*Naked* takes us to The Beginning. Only the elites became Christian; NOBODY else could understand the game of it. This was

Abraham *with* Sarah's young handmaiden; we are told that in his mind, this was something *God* suggested him to do. There wasn't any lightning flashing down, no angel appeared to stop a much older man."

"No angel appeared from another dimension to stop King David from his various antics, either."

"Jack Parsons launched Jet Propulsion Lab and the Aerospace Corporation. He hired beautiful women, and Jack had sex with them all, over fifty in total, like King David's many wives, according to those who counted. Other men worked there, but they are like the disciples who stayed in the boat, while Jack is like Peter, who asks if he can walk on the water."

"Jack Parsons possessed no special powers to pick-up women, but understood the Bible in the same way that people can snap their fingers. Jack understood that Jesus was *clarifying* what Adam and Eve had missed, that we are supposed to encounter every little thing we face as fresh, all new, as *ourselves*, and this was how he approached women, as *himself*. Then the women around him understood that he had *a unique capacity*."

"*Capacity* within the person is what *attracts,* the space *between* the beats carries the magnetism."

"Jack tested-out this theory *of* himself, and if you haven't tested it, don't knock it."

"We notice that when they came to arrest Jesus, Peter is the one who picked up a sword to defend him and Jesus had to override Peter. And Peter was the one who denied Jesus, but this is what it takes to shed the social program; it's a journey fraught with missteps."

"Jesus said to 'the accusers of the woman,' 'Let him who is without sin cast the first stone.' What he meant, was to allow others their own *timeline* to make their own mistakes; Jesus was like the loving mother who believes in her own children no matter what."

"Jesus is geometry, plus a fourth dimension, or that 'point in space' which shifts one perspective into something else," Jack told Thumbert.

"The Apostle Peter tested-out this theory that he could walk on water too. Jesus affirmed Peter while he was in the boat, while it was Peter who picked-up a sword, while Peter also denied Jesus. Ordinary mortals are each on a journey, and if you haven't tested it out by taking your own journey, and by making a few serious mistakes, don't knock it."

"In the religion of a bureaucracy, nobody gets to take their own journey; only to follow in another's path. Abraham had no previous model to copy, to have intercourse with the handmaiden, so we could say that he was a man who had an original idea. Out of that, the people *without* an original idea missed the point."

"Joseph followed Abraham's example, and Joseph's special thing was that he wore a coat of many colors. This too must have been an original idea, showing us that the brothers, without an original idea, dug a deep hole in the ground, threw Joseph into it."

"Jesus says, that not a single sparrow falls without the Father knowing, so if we put ourselves into the shoes of Jack Parsons, we'd need to snap our fingers to appreciate what this means; get the meaning fast, don't think too long."

"We live within an all-knowing field of energy."

"A sparrow is not a thing, but an interruption within the broader field of energy, which is sparrow-consciousness."

"God would have to be interdimensional, so when the sparrow falls, this represents two dimensions: "what is," and "what was." To higher-energy dimensions of broader perspective, these are both the same, said Parsons. He asked, how many dimensions are out there?"

"Humans reside within one dimension, while God has no such limitations."

"Certain interesting drugs can cross humans into other dimensions, made illegal, of course."

"When Jesus walks on the water, he was demonstrating the fields of dimensions, while the boat represents the solid dimension, and this is where most ordinary people live, such as the disciples of Jesus, so Jesus must train them *out* of their dimensionality, but each person must *ask* for such training or it doesn't just happen; hence we have the other disciples in the boat."

"Jesus must train the brothers of Joseph *out-of* throwing others into deep holes, to have a little more imagination than that. Thus, it is Jesus in Heaven who gets the last laugh, after Joseph is the one who saves his brothers from starvation."

"It was Peter who said he was willing to put it to the test, which he does, by making a request. The average person interprets that Peter was merely walking on water, like Jesus was, but it blew Peter's mind. True spiritual growth shows itself by blowing our minds."

"To have one's mind blown, it requires that one makes the request, then watch, and wait, which sometimes requires only twenty, thirty seconds, then we step-out of the boat."

What Thumbert saw in Jack Parsons, was not some sort of rocket propulsion scientist employed by the military/industrial complex, but somebody who could snap his fingers and get straight to the point. Rocket-propulsion genius came to him as a byproduct of his learning to practice magic. Having sex with the female staff at Aerospace was likewise a byproduct of something else he had going on.

"Jack Parsons was not a clone of anybody else, never turned anybody into his clone; this never crossed his mind."

Sleeping with beautiful women was Parson's experiment, not an end in itself. It's about creating miracles in your own life apart from hierarchical considerations, which says, "Don't do it."

This is how Marjorie Cameron came to knock on Parson's door, after Parsons conjured her as the complete stranger from across the energetic dimensions, then locked her into a room and had sex with her nonstop for two weeks. Marjorie Cameron was Parson's confirmation of the spiritual dimension; had nothing to do with his carnal self; he was already in anticipation of her when the doorbell rang. "Oh to have been a fly on the wall," Thumbert said, because this was something he could not have done.

Then Thumbert met Jack Parsons, because Thumbert was on this same journey, while everybody else was stuck within the realm of one-dimension. Thumbert said that there are not many people who can reside outside the normal dimensions, but the ones who are, attract each other like magnets.

And then Yolita met Jack Parsons and Thumbert left her in the care of Marjorie Cameron.

Jack P. told Yolita she was photogenic,
then she jumped on this ladder.
"Oh really? Photogenic?"
was written on the back by Cameron.
California, April, 1952

What Jack Parsons had in common with Jack Kennedy: It was their mothers who taught them that they could get *out* of the boat to walk on the water. Then it is THE MOTHERS who must meet their child brought back from the war, lying dead on their own shield.

"Even the consciousness of the sparrow, will not fall from its flight between the dimensions, so take the risk, and take the challenge; if you are a mother, teach this," Thumbert said.

Now Yolita had little appreciation for how she had gotten from Iowa to California, which is why Thumbert wanted to write his book in 1953, because it REQUIRED an entire book, for her (and her generation) to understand what the hell was going on.

Thumbert mentioned once that Charmin Hayes was not doing the proper job *of a mother*.

Thus, he accepted Yolita as a form of nurture, as a challenge to him, as a father figure.

Thumbert told me that he had explained all of the intricate detail about Jack Parsons while he was in jail, especially the magical Jesus-dimension parts tied to rocketry, while the two men questioning him at the prison, after Thumbert gave his longwinded lecture, laughed.

Thumbert asked: "Is it the backstory, required to get to the real story? Is this what they have no patience to hear? When it's all so simple?"

The Intelligence Service's invention of Thumbert as Humbert

The backstory seems to last forever, then snap your fingers, the story is over, while yes, another story begins.

Chapter 54

Translatio imperii.

John Nearly.

Certain events have transpired, such that my time for this world is short.

What I mean is, that no matter who you are, no matter how long you grace this planet, your time here will be short. All men are condemned to death.

Let's not kid ourselves.

Below are some additional lecture notes I had typed, following Thumbert's lectures, for whatever value you might find. I'd work these notes into chapters; just fit them in yourself wherever it makes sense to you and good luck in all you do.

John B. Nearly

Des Moines, Iowa

January 22, 1963

Chapter 55

Additional Thumbert Lecture Notes:

He kissed the plump mellow yellow smellow melons of her rump, on each plump melonous hemisphere, in their mellow yellow furrow, with obscure prolonged provocative melonsmellonous osculation.
--James Joyce

Let's get to the heart of what I wanted to say because humanity is not very good at looking back to question what worked and what did not work.

For example, in 1492, Columbus sailed the ocean blue.

How did that go? Where's the customer feedback?

My compatriots within the bureau have asked me several times: What is Thumbert's FAITH?

Jew, Catholic, Protestant? Zen Buddhist?

Why they care, if they know a man's faith, they can then relax, that he is not *godless* nor a communist.

And yet, we don't want some kind of religious FANATIC in the West and even the pope must be careful on this count. Religion is okay with the people as long as everybody remains calm.

"Ask what you want if you are a Christian," Thumbert said.

"If you are not a Christian, ask anyway."

Most people can see that there are two kinds of Christians, or Jews or Muslims: the ones who attend a religious service on a certain day of the week and then there's the absolutists.

Absolutists rail upon the magic-parts, turn us away from the miracles, set Jesus out of reachj.

This is why religions are written in languages few can read or understand.

We are told that the Roman emperor Nero was throwing the new Christians to the lions during the First Century church. Did he? "Nero" did that because every single one of the apostles was an absolutist. Were they? Early Christianity was not calm by any standard. If so, what was there to get excited about? Forgiven *sins*? Or the sudden realization that everybody was free to be themselves?

Why were the Germans the egalitarians? and not the Catholics officially egalitarian? Was Vatican City egalitarian only behind closed dorrs?

This ancient tapestry starts to unravel as soon as we ask questions.

Cuba is communist?

Words and terms are coming apart at the seams.

27

26

I'll get straight to the point. In short order, trust me, I will.

Arminius. September, 9 AD. The Battle of Teutoburg Forest. What was the crime? The double-cross of Rome's legions or simply an inspiration, leading to Hitler.

Hitler. September, 1939. Blitzkrieg on Poland. What was the crime? Profiteering or simply becoming an inspiration.

Martin Luther. September, 1517. The Wittenberg Door. What was the crime?

Odoacer. September, 476 AD. The Fall of Rome, again. What was the crime?

Constantine, Fourth Century, Official Adoption of Christianity, What was the crime? The launching of a new form of interrogation?

(Note to self. Lavrently Beria, Kremlin complex as architecture, date built?

Alexandria, DC, Virginia, obelisks

We were discussing Allen Dulles, an attorney with the prestigious law firm, Sullivan & Cromwell, who became a kind of International spy with the OSS during WWII under Roosevelt.

And that Sullivan & Cromwell's corporate clients were the most prestigious, international in scope, so it would be pretty cool if an attorney from S&C could sneak into a neutral country in 1945, like Switzerland, to negotiate a kind of German surrender behind Hitler's back to save whatever German corporations who happened to be clients of Sullivan & Cromwell from falling into the hands of the Russian communists.

And that Allen's brother, John Foster, likewise was an attorney with Sullivan & Cromwell, who somehow mbecomes Secretary of State under Eisenhower.

And how is that going to work after Eisenhower w/o nixon ?

Because A system of self-perpetuation is being establisheed and who could have seen it coming?

Like all these LOOSE THREADS need to be woven back into the tapestry following the end of War in Europe, and who better for the job, if not Sullivan & Cromwell, representing clients at some fairly high levels?

Otherwise known as "the revolving door btwn industry and (the right kind of)egalitarian political monied ambition.

We need a better word for what Sullivan & Cromwell was doing,other than *capitalism*.

27

This has been wracking my brain.

Who actually has been hijackng the U.S. government and other gov'ts worldwide?

Not the mafia

1962 is like some kind of a pimple and pimple creme.

28

I heard him say it twice, maybe three times. How young Catherine de' Medici of Italy and Henry of France were brought together by the pope. Fourteen-year-olds.

The very morning after official ceremony, while the very young royal couple is very likely still naked, and asleep, the pope, he does not knock, just enters, to check, yes, okay, all good. Has the marriage been consummated?

Catherine asks, "Holy Father, what do I *do*?"

The pope replies, "Lay, lady, *lay*! Lay across his big brass bed."

She asks, "And what shall I think about?"

The Holy Father replies, "Whatever colors you have in your mind, he'll show them to you, and you'll see them shine."

Catherine says, "Holy Father, I had a bad dream last night. I saw a black branch with blood that kept dripping."

The pope said, "Why wait any longer for the world to begin? You can have your cake and eat it too. Stay with your man a while, see if you can make himsmile. Then, I'll be back."

"Thank you, Holy Father."

27

One time early on, while sitting with Thumbert, my whisky drained from my glass, ice half-melted, too tired to fix another, Thumbert's voice droning on, my eyes grew so heavy.

Suddenly, he was addressing me, tapping his pipe, leaning forward, gazing upon my slumbered corpse. He asked me, "Do you think I'm just waxing poetic?"

In my brain there were no words.

Thumbert said to me, "Go fuckv yourself."

I had heard him say this to Yolita once, "Do you think I am just waxing poetic?"

Yolita likewise, staring back at him.

He said, "Go fuck yourself, Yolita."

She asked me once, "Johnny, do you think I am waxing poetic?"

She said, "Then go vfuck yourself, Johnny."

I appreciated in that moment that Yolita loved Thumbert as much as I did.

28

The reason why the King of England ended war with the American colonialists, was that the Founding Fathers agreed to tell their story in such a way that did not discredit the king. The Founding Fathers then noted for the history books that their revolution was caused by a tax on their tea.

Thumbert imitated in a high British accent: "A tax on their tea?"

29

Thumbert once asked me, "Where is our evidence for Moses?"

"He is in the scriptures."

"I see," he replied as if deep in thought, after observing how quickly I had answered: "That is very interesting."

"Was Moses a king?"

"No," I replied.

He asked, "So the Jews had no king?"

What a great model. Always look at a person's shoes, Thumbert advised

This is what our minds give us all day long, explanations.

Parsons pulled Marjorie Cameron inside by the hand, they had sex nonstop for two weeks; which is how it was intended and goddamnit Jack needed not explain himself to me .

29

So I was angry now. I said, "Thumbert, you make sense of what you lecture because you know more than you are telling, this to that, and that to this, this begets that, and so on. Just spill it! Tell me what you are trying to say!"

",. You are an HERESY, John. Your lifetime is nothing but a delay of the inevitable Not just you but everybody else who gets in your way. The question is, what are you going to do about it?"

"God can do anything which blows our minds except He can't keep track of all the shit that's been going on. After a while, it's just too fucking uninteresting. We're not immoral Johnny; we're just super uninteresting creatures, rarely com e up with an original thought, and God has no time for it. I'd move on, can't blame God for this, wouldn you?"

" You don't need to explain yourself to me, Johnny, don't need your personal data."

30

Jack Parsonsm n= MAGIC the Jews magic the Ashkenazi no king Hitler Stalin

We can sum Thumbert's from here as free love but how.

Russian succession and grafts hay barns tractors.

American succession grafts, the hamburger, soft bun in particular, pickles

French grafts succession, various hats, flat ones, high, wide

Roman succession. Caesar, cleo, Vespasian jews.

Jesus, David, succession, Abraham, God's blessing

I will love whom I will love Calvinist Huguenots

Dulles and the cold war and I'd suppose jack Kennedy, Joe & Rose K.

History of protestants, Shakespeare

It gets interesting, Thumbert said.

J. Edgar Hoover.

study of Napoleon, death, cannons, propulsion, area 57, cathedrals, energy.

Thumbert never made headlines,\

under my thumb, etc., news, etc. lyrics, C IA, Humbert, Universal Pictures, etc.

Surely Nabokov was exposed to the news of his day.

Nabokov

Victor Hugo, the poet is the revolutionary.

Yolita being homely as a boy/girl
John based in iowa \=
Sasquatch hiding in state parks, national parks
Hangar 18
We are here to help you
Heinrich in Prague
Kennedy runup
James joyce melon quote
Yesss
Stalin show me the man and I'll show you the crime. Lavrently Beria, longest servicing secret police chief 1941-53 detention for political prisoners
Attention is the greatest currency.

Two tiers

Cowboys vs choir boys

Operation dandelion

Donovan vs Nuremburg

aspirin

Special thanks to

Mark Groubert and Eric Hunley, Jon Levi, and James Bradley.

Bob Dylan, Neil Young, Buffalo Springfield, CSN&Y, and REM.

Lucius Aurelian and Leksa Biffer, t.y.

The end.

Author Bio

Scott W. Webb

The author has written numerous books on a variety of topics, available on Amazon.

Website: www.colonicexpert.com.

Made in the USA
Columbia, SC
03 February 2024

30981399R00113